A Complaint Is a Gift Workbook

101 Activities, Exercises, and Tools to Learn from Critical Feedback and Recover Customer Loyalty

Janelle Barlow and Victoria Holtz

BK

Berrett–Koehler Publishers, Inc.

Berrett-Koehler Publishers, Inc.
1333 Broadway, Suite 1000
Oakland, CA 94612-1921
Tel: (510) 817-2277
Fax: (510) 817-2278
www.bkconnection.com

ORDERING INFORMATION

Quantity sales. Special discounts are available on quantity purchases by corporations, associations, and others. For details, contact the "Special Sales Department" at the Berrett-Koehler address above.
Individual sales. Berrett-Koehler publications are available through most bookstores. They can also be ordered directly from Berrett-Koehler: Tel: (800) 929-2929; Fax: (802) 864-7626; www.bkconnection.com.
Orders for college textbook / course adoption use. Please contact Berrett-Koehler: Tel: (800) 929-2929; Fax: (802) 864-7626.

Distributed to the U.S. trade and internationally by Penguin Random House Publisher Services.

Berrett-Koehler and the BK logo are registered trademarks of Berrett-Koehler Publishers, Inc.

Illustrations are used per a license agreement with Getty Images.

Printed in the United States of America

Berrett-Koehler books are printed on long-lasting acid-free paper. When it is available, we choose paper that has been manufactured by environmentally responsible processes. These may include using trees grown in sustainable forests, incorporating recycled paper, minimizing chlorine in bleaching, or recycling the energy produced at the paper mill.

Library of Congress Cataloging-in-Publication Data

Names: Barlow, Janelle, 1943- author. | Holtz, Victoria, author.
Title: A complaint is a gift workbook : 101 activities, exercises, and
  tools to learn from critical feedback and recover customer loyalty /
  Janelle Barlow, Victoria Holtz.
Description: First Edition. | Oakland, CA : Berrett-Koehler Publishers,
  [2023]
Identifiers: LCCN 2022018519 (print) | LCCN 2022018520 (ebook) | ISBN
  9781523002979 (paperback) | ISBN 9781523002986 (pdf) | ISBN
  9781523003013 (epub)
Subjects: LCSH: Consumer complaints. | Customer services.
Classification: LCC HF5415.52 .B374 2023 (print) | LCC HF5415.52 (ebook)
  | DDC 658.8/343—dc23/eng/20220729
LC record available at https://lccn.loc.gov/2022018519
LC ebook record available at https://lccn.loc.gov/2022018520

First Edition
30 29 28 27 26 25 24 23 22   10 9 8 7 6 5 4 3 2 1

Book producer and copyeditor: PeopleSpeak
Text designer: Reider Books
Cover designer: Frances Baca

This Workbook is dedicated to

every hard-working complaint handler who

interacts with customers to make things right,

remains cool under pressure,

delights customers,

respects even difficult customers,

and still wants to get better at turning dissatisfied

complainers into happy, long-term promoters.

We celebrate you!

Contents

Preface

What if we saw complaints as gifts? What if we said "Thank you" whenever we received such a gift? How would the whole field of complaint handling change?

Do you find it hard to handle complaints or destructive feedback that someone has thrown at you? You're not alone. Most people have difficulty with negative feedback. That's why we've written this workbook, to make complaint handling effortless and pleasing for you and a lot more beneficial to your organization. We wrote this guide so you can see complaints as gifts!

This workbook is a companion to the book *A Complaint Is a Gift* by Janelle Barlow, which covers some of the same ideas we will go through here. But this workbook is focused on practical techniques— the how-to of complaint handling. It closes the gap between theory and application. This hands-on guide shows how to perform well at one of the most challenging jobs.

Many people assume that all Customer Service Representatives (CSRs) need to be knowledgeable only about the products they represent. They think that since people have been receiving negative feedback throughout their lives, they must know more or less how to handle complaints. That's not true. Ask CSRs about the most challenging part of complaint handling, and they'll tell you they can get information about products, but they frequently don't have any idea how to handle a customer who is irate, is not able to settle down, or threatens to talk with someone higher up in the organization.

This workbook is filled with both fun and challenging activities to handle these difficult situations. To be precise, we've included 101 activities! We're sure you will find at least a few dozen that will work precisely for you, and the rest will let you see the variety of complaints that CSRs receive. This will provide you with multiple options to better interact with complaining customers.

But besides making it possible to get through life without falling apart from negative feedback, why should you care about better complaint handling?

If customers don't like the way their complaints are handled, one of the easiest ways for them to react is to leave a business. If they don't personally like the way they were treated, they can let thousands know exactly what happened by going online.

Talking with dissatisfied customers may be the most important communication CSRs have. It's a chance to improve business by fixing problems. Even more remarkable, if they fix a problem for customers and treat them well, their customers will likely develop stronger loyalty to the business.

It pays to do everything you can to keep customers satisfied and happy—and not only customers but also employees, including you.

Experimenting with complaint-handling techniques will let you choose from various approaches. You'll become more agile in dealing with different types of customers. You'll get better at organizing your work around the concept that listening to your customers and encouraging them to speak out when they see something wrong is a good idea. You'll also learn to pay attention to that critical point in the customer-service process when things go wrong.

We'll help you fill in gaps in your knowledge so you can carry your new skills into any future work you undertake, whether as an employee or an entrepreneur. As a result, you will no doubt become more customer focused. Everyone will benefit as well: you as a Customer Service Representative, your customers, your team, and your organization.

Our intention here is to step into your life and show how you can provide customer support, love what you do, and learn how to handle difficult customer interactions, or any other type of negative feedback.

Complaints and Gifts

Welcome to a journey of self-discovery, with practical tools and case examples that will help you master handling feedback and complaints. We'll introduce you to a mindset about complaint handling that will help you improve relationships at work and in your personal life. We're going to introduce you to the A Complaint Is a Gift philosophy!

Who This Workbook Is For

This workbook is for everyone who wants to learn more about giving and constructively receiving feedback. It's specifically for complaint handlers, but you will find it has value for service providers, salespeople, managers, team members, and trainers as well as people who don't like personal criticism.

This workbook can also help organizations run internal workshops to strengthen complaint-handling competencies of both leaders and employees. You can find the A Complaint Is a Gift (CIAG) Train the Trainers program on our web page. You can join this private trainer group and attend quarterly live sessions with us. We also share recommendations to excel at delivering CIAG in-house programs using the contents of this workbook.

We did not write this workbook for managers or supervisors who guide teams of complaint handlers. Nonetheless, they will find it valuable so they can operate with the same understanding as their teams.

We wrote this workbook to delve into the business of customer feedback that many complaint handlers know only at a cursory level. Of course, that's not true for all complaint handlers. Some have years of experience and have completed excellent training. However, these people may be rarer than you think. Most CSRs have been trained to be friendly and helpful but are instructed to more or less handle complaints in a way that focuses on an organization's processes rather than its customers.

If you are a CSR, you are incredibly valuable to your organization's bottom line because your primary responsibility is bringing customers to a state of satisfaction and loyalty after they have faced a problem. We believe CSR turnover would happen far less often if complaint handlers were empowered to use their creativity to find reasonable and fair problem solutions for their customers.

Barring these changes occurring, we believe the explanations and techniques offered in this workbook will have a great impact on job performance. Some readers may find all 101 activities don't exactly fit their precise job description, but going through those exercises, whether or not they fit your job description, will help you understand the principles we cover. We have written this workbook to cover a broad range of CSRs dealing with a wide variety of customer issues. We advise readers to feel free to make adjustments in specific examples but not miss the bigger points being made.

Working with a Partner

You will at times be asked to do an activity with another person. Think about someone with whom you would like to work. They can go through these same materials or not. A partner will enable you to get someone else's reactions. They can push you with their responses, particularly when you ask them to play the role of a customer.

Abbreviations and Terms Used in This Workbook

As much as we like the phrase "A Complaint Is a Gift," it contains seventeen letters, plus four spaces, so you will see the abbreviation CIAG.

You will see also LTIO, an abbreviation that appears with almost every activity. It means "Let's Try It Out." It's an invitation for you to jump in and do something. This could involve answering a question, taking an assessment, or reviewing a lesson you have covered.

You'll also see "Learning Point," which indicates an important point emphasized in that activity.

We'll also use the abbreviation CSR, meaning Customer Service Representative. Just remember, whatever your company calls your job position (e.g., CSRs, service providers, complaint handlers, product exchange staff, computer techs), this book speaks to all workers who handle complaints as all or some part of their job responsibilities.

Self-Checks

After each chapter, except for chapter 1, you will find a self-check. It's a chance to review what you have covered up to that point and reinforce what you have learned. Please don't skip these self-checks because they will help you better retain all the content we cover.

Graphical Images

We have worked hard to insert images that represent the broad range of students of this material. Most of the images come from Getty Images, the world's largest commercial image archive, unless otherwise specified. We appreciate the value these images add to this workbook.

How to Use Accompanying Blended Resources

As you start this workbook, we ask you to make some commitments—that you will do the activities, answer the questionnaires, complete the assessments, and use the interactive tools. Any learning experience requires trying things out. This workbook is meant to be a journey of self-discovery to improve your skills in a fun, proven, and practical way.

You are more than welcome to go through this workbook in the order in which it is presented. You can also get creative and skip around, though you will find ideas are grouped together in chapters and are probably best learned together. If you clearly know the content, feel free to skip some of the activities, but they can also offer a chance to review the concepts.

In several activities, you will see links to our web page www.ciag .online/. There you will find many resources.

As a bonus for purchasing the workbook, you can join our A Complaint Is a Gift Facebook group, which is filled with even more resources as well as live events with us and our guests. It's a brilliant community. Members share knowledge and on-time recommendations to expand your learning and keep you up to date on the latest complaint-handling trends and tactics. It's a field that is constantly changing.

URLs and Links

URLs and links sometimes change or get corrupted, especially You-Tube video links. If you find a link to referenced material, videos, or pages that no longer works, please send us an email. We'll treat your complaint as a gift and will be happy to send you updated links or the direct material. Please contact us at info@AComplaintIsAGift.com.

Welcome from Your Guides

A quick welcome from Victoria and Janelle. You'll learn more about us as you progress through this workbook, and you can read about our backgrounds at the back of this book.

But for the moment, we want to extend our hellos. We're excited to guide you through the process of paying attention to that critical point in the customer-service process when things go wrong. With this focus, you will no doubt attend more closely to your customers, and your service recovery will automatically become more customer centric. This, in turn, will enhance your role in focusing on your customers for your company or business.

We're happy to walk through this journey with you.

CHAPTER 1

Getting Started

Any successful journey requires direction, guides, and a plan. We are delighted to help you start your learning journey by asking— no, insisting!—that you commit to your own success.

Then you will be invited to set your starting point by taking a self-assessment. This assessment can be repeated several times as you go through the workbook to track your improvements. How often you do this is up to you. But we strongly urge you, at a minimum, to repeat this assessment at the conclusion of the workbook.

You'll make progress as you go along. This process may sound simple, even though it isn't. Complaint handling is complex. But when it works well, it's very rewarding!

My Commitment to Success

You are here! It's time to start this learning experience. This means you are taking a big step to improve your complaint-handling skills. Congratulations!

LTIO: To get ready, we recommend you study this list of tasks and put a check in each box that you commit to. These choices will enhance your learning process. Come back every once in a while so you can make sure you are following through.

- ☐ Schedule time to work on this workbook. Control interruptions.
- ☐ Choose a comfortable place to read and do the activities.
- ☐ Have your computer, smartphone, or tablet nearby to watch the videos, and complete similar activities.
- ☐ Do the activities in order or skip around.
- ☐ Be ready to stretch. Some activities will get you out of your comfort zone.
- ☐ Be honest. The activities are just for you. No one is checking.
- ☐ Join our Facebook community for more perks and monthly enhancement sessions.
- ☐ Advance at your own pace.
- ☐ Use colored markers or highlighters to grab your attention.
- ☐ If you like, have your favorite food and beverage at hand so you can stimulate your senses.

ACTIVITY

2

What's My Starting Point?

We assume you want to show improvement in your complaint handling. You would probably also like to feel good at the end of your work shift—and so would your customers.

We'll start with a self-assessment about your complaint behaviors. You can also take this assessment after you have gone through this workbook to see what changes you have made. We're confident you will have made improvements.

Complaint handling is complex. But when it works well, it's remarkable. If your customers walk away happy and satisfied, you'll finish your shift feeling you contributed to others and have energy for other parts of your life.

LTIO: Go to a self-assessment quiz at www.ciag.online/2 where you will assess yourself on a scale from 1 to 5.

Notes:

_____

_____

_____

_____

_____

_____

_____

CHAPTER 2

Understanding Complaints

A lot of people don't like complaints at all. To them, they see only trouble at their doorstep. But it's a mistake to automatically see a problem. Some complaints are opportunities in disguise, and sometimes a complaint is resolved in a way that causes people to get closer to each other. In family groups, that happens a lot.

In business, we will define a complaint as a direct statement about expectations that haven't been met. When expectations aren't met, customers become dissatisfied, and we run the risk of losing them.

In this chapter, we'll look at what complaints are and give you a chance to define how you see complaints.

ACTIVITY

3

What Is a Complaint to You?

We can think about complaints in multiple ways. Understanding your personal view of customer feedback will enable you to know what, if anything, needs to shift for you to adopt a mindset that sees complaints as gifts.

There are no right or wrong ways to complete these exercises. The best answer is to provide a honest, robust picture of how you think about complaints. You won't get extra points by writing down what you think we want you to say.

1. What five words come to mind when you hear the word *complaint*? Write them down on the lines below. Then rate each word positive, negative, or neutral.

   1. _____
      Positive   Negative   Neutral

   2. _____
      Positive   Negative   Neutral

   3. _____
      Positive   Negative   Neutral

   4. _____
      Positive   Negative   Neutral

   5. _____
      Positive   Negative   Neutral

2. Draw a picture of a complaint.

[ ]

3. Look at the words you chose in the first question. Do they match your picture? Yes ___ No ___ Sort of ___

LTIO: What do these three exercises tell you about your perceptions of complaints?

_____

_____

_____

Feedback versus Complaints

You are likely to see a sign or statement that says "We want your feedback" in many places in different forms and formats. It's a good sign that asks, "Tell us what you think."

However, even though we've been looking everywhere for years, we have yet to see a sign that says "We want your complaints." If you see such a sign, please send us an image of it!

These two words—*feedback* and *complaints*—are frequently used interchangeably. Perhaps you use them in much the same way. That's just fine. At times in this workbook, you will see that we swap the terms too.

According to Merriam-Webster's dictionary, feedback is a reaction or response to something. That definition doesn't help distinguish the two words because a reaction or response could also be a complaint.

Our definition of *complaints* is more precise. A complaint is a statement about expectations that have not been met. A complaint expresses dissatisfaction. *Feedback*, however, doesn't necessarily mean that you are dissatisfied.

It helps if you think about feedback as either positive or negative. We don't think of complaints that way. If a statement is considered to be a complaint, it means it is negative. When we hear negative feedback, we typically don't call it a complaint. It's just feedback.

While the techniques in this workbook cover how to handle complaints, you can also use them for negative feedback. We aren't going to discuss how to handle positive feedback. We think you know how to do that!

LTIO: How do you distinguish between the two terms? Give examples.

Feedback: _____

_____

_____

Complaints: _____

_____

_____

Notes:

_____

_____

_____

_____

_____

_____

_____

_____

_____

_____

_____

_____

_____

_____

_____

My Best Complaint

Some complaints or feedback are among the best gifts we will ever receive. Many times, we don't recognize that a complaint is a gift—let alone accept it as a good event in our lives. It may take months or even years to recognize that it was a gift.

LTIO: First, think of a complaint you received when you knew you would benefit from the feedback right away. Describe what happened. Indicate how you were able to see that the complaint was going to benefit you; for example, was it the delivery or the content?

_____

_____

Second, think of a complaint that started off as a really bad complaint but under further consideration became your best complaint because it gave you the most value. Please describe it in the space below.

_____

_____

Third, what changed so that you now consider it a positive event in your life? Did you incorporate what you learned from this feedback?

_____

_____

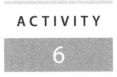

My Worst Complaint

You have probably heard some really bad customer complaints. This feedback may have been so bad you can hardly remember it because you want so desperately to forget what was said or what happened.

LTIO: Consider the worst complaint you've heard directed at you personally or at your company. This complaint or piece of feedback still bothers you, makes you angry, or generates a feeling of unfairness. Describe it in the space below. What made it such bad feedback? Was it the way it was delivered, or was it because of the content?

_____

_____

_____

What do you think would have to change for you to consider it a positive event in your life?

_____

_____

_____

That's what this workbook and its activities are designed to do: to turn your customer complaints quickly into gifts so you don't have to wait days, weeks, or even years for that to happen.

Why Do I Complain?

We all have our personal reasons why we complain. Sometimes it's because of what some other person does or says. Other times it has to do with us—maybe we're tired or hungry. Or perhaps we've been putting up with too much for us to handle, and we are easily irritated. That's when we complain.

Most of us can look back at times when we've complained and regret that we did. Other times we wish we had spoken up. Do you think our customers ever feel that way? It's a fine line we walk whether to complain or not.

Of course, we all complain—at least sometimes. But let's start with *you*.

LTIO: List three reasons why you complain. Your examples can be either from home or work.

1. _____

2. _____

3. _____

Can you list a couple more examples? A nice, long list can help you understand why deciding to complain—or not—can be complex and varied, which in turn helps us see why someone complains to us.

1. _____

2. _____

Why do you think it's important to complain?

_____

_____

_____

Note: When you start any of these activities and run out of ideas, you can put them aside and come back to your work later. Sometimes a little time off will give you even better ideas.

Notes:

_____

_____

_____

_____

_____

_____

_____

_____

_____

_____

_____

_____

_____

Who Has the Right to Complain?

Have you ever complained unfairly? Let's explain what we mean by that with a real-life example from Victoria:

> On the day before Christmas, my parents and siblings were invited to lunch. My husband was not happy as he had many things to do that day, including all of us going to dinner at his family's house. He was worried we would be late and exhausted after hosting eighteen members of my family for lunch. I must confess I complained, "Why is your side of the family more important than mine?"
>
> Do you think that was a valid complaint? Have you ever said the same or similar thing?
>
> Of course, that complaint was not fair. But it got worse. I asked him to help set the table; he said no, he needed to go handle something. I got really angry. "What? Where? Why now? I need you here!" He just looked at me and left. When he came back, I had set the table and handled all the luncheon arrangements. He said, "Great, I see it's all done! I brought ice."
>
> What would you have felt if you were me? What would you have told him? What would be your next complaint?
>
> I stared at him and said, "Yes, I did it, no thanks to you!" We had a stressful lunch, and the tension spread between us even at Christmas dinner. The next morning, we rushed to open gifts. There were almost none by the tree the night before, but it

was piled high with boxes of all sizes in the morning. Our kids were surprised and delighted. Then my husband said, "Do you remember I said I had things to do yesterday? I had to pick up and wrap all the gifts and put them in the storage room so the kids wouldn't see them."

Let's look carefully at this scenario. Has something like this ever happened to you? How do you think Victoria felt at that moment?

Here's the most important question: did Victoria have the right to complain when she did? From her point of view, she clearly had the right. Maybe she could have been more sensitive to her husband. But did she have the *right* to complain?

LTIO: Obviously, her husband could have handled her complaint better as well. What could he have done better? Jot down a couple of ideas.

1. _____

2. _____

What did you think about when reading this anecdote? What would you say to Victoria? What might have helped her resolve a common family complaint even though she had the right to complain?

1. _____

2. _____

3. _____

What three ideas did you consider while going through this activity that might help you resolve a similar kind of complaint?

1. _____

2. _____

3. _____

LEARNING POINT: We all have the right to complain—even if what we complain about might have been made without sufficient information.

Notes:

_____

_____

_____

_____

_____

_____

_____

_____

_____

_____

_____

_____

ACTIVITY

9

Why Don't I Complain?

Sometimes we have good reasons to complain, and yet we don't say a word. That makes us one of the 96 percent of customers who don't complain about relatively unimportant items. Obviously, if we have a severe issue, such as if the tires on our newly purchased car fall off, we speak up. But we often eat soup that is too salty, we drink warm beer, or we leave the fish that tastes too fishy. Why do we do this?

Sometimes we think, "I'm certain they're trying their best," "If I complain, the cook may spit on my food when they take my dish back to the kitchen to reheat," or "It's such a small thing, I'm not going to say anything," so we keep quiet.

LTIO: In situations like the ones above, do you complain? Always? Under what three circumstances when you are a customer do you not complain? Why?

1. _____

2. _____

3. _____

Let's take an example from your personal or work life about a friend or colleague. Do you always complain about what you don't like about someone else's behavior? Why or why not?

1. _____

2. _____

3. _____

Even if we don't say anything, we probably are at least annoyed when people do things we don't like. But we don't tell them we dislike it. Think about it: how can they become aware and change this behavior if we don't tell them?

Here are a few reasons why people say they don't complain:

- "I complained before and nothing changed."
- "I didn't want to hurt the other person's feelings."
- "I was afraid of losing that person's love or good feelings."
- "I was afraid of physical retaliation."
- "I didn't want to hear any nasty, defensive comments from them."

LTIO: Think of two people who did something that you did not complain about but would like to give feedback to. Write down their names. What is that feedback? When will you tell them?

Avoid complaining about things that can't change (e.g., "I don't like how tall you are"). The person can't do anything about that! Choose something that affects you and is important to you.

Name of Person 1 : _____

Feedback: _____

When: _____

Name of Person 2: _____

Feedback: _____

When: _____

After you've given feedback to two people, share with a partner what happened with those people you complained to. With your partner, explore how it felt to complain and whether you'd try it again. We will explore this topic more in chapter 13.

ACTIVITY

10

To Complain or Not—It's Complex

During the COVID-19 pandemic, Janelle visited urgent care multiple times and had five additional doctor's visits, which involved seeing an orthopedic doctor and getting three sets of x-rays to check for broken bones. She had a deteriorating condition with her right foot. Doctors sent her home each time, saying, "We don't know what's wrong."

Janelle ultimately suffered a complete rupture of her anterior tibialis. If you look up this tendon, you will see that splitting it is not good. Even though she could hobble around, it was clear that her foot was not working. Finally she was referred to an orthopedic surgeon outside her primary care hospital, who diagnosed the problem within seconds of looking at her foot. An MRI confirmed that she needed a cadaver tendon replacement because her tendon had ruptured and separated by eight inches.

All of Janelle's friends have asked, "How did you let it go on so long before the tendon replacement surgery had to be done?"

This is where complaining gets complicated. Did Janelle complain? Yes, to many people. Did she complain to the doctors where she went for care? Nope. None of them.

It seems that if she ever had an occasion to complain, this was it. Yet she didn't speak up. Janelle feels some personal responsibility for not protesting louder while her tendon was merely injured and when a minor fix might have sufficed. She knew nothing about this tendon and took the word of every doctor she saw. She accepted x-rays telling her no bones were broken and that she should "go home and take it easy." The problem was that she didn't have a broken bone.

Janelle has sympathy for her doctors as all this occurred during the pandemic years, and she was willing to cut her medical personnel some slack. She even accepted a painful cortisone shot in the tendon before its complete rupture, which she later learned through a Google search should not be done on a torn tendon.

After a second visit to urgent care, during which she waited hours in unbelievably intense pain, she received a ten-point Net Promoter Score survey to complete about her treatment quality. Janelle gave them a rating of three. The following week she received a telephone call asking if she would like to change that rating to something higher. Janelle instead suggested they change the care unit's name from "urgent care" to "slow care."

You may be thinking, "But isn't this the same Janelle who wrote three editions of a book called *A Complaint Is a Gift*?" Yes, she is. And yet, here she was, not complaining about surgery that demanded six weeks with zero pressure on her foot—and facing a long recovery. It required a full year before her foot remembered how to behave, and she will have an eight-inch scar running up the top of her foot as a perpetual reminder.

Janelle offers her story so you can understand why people don't complain, which may include you. Complaining or not complaining is a highly individual and complex emotional decision.

Early research about what percentage of people complain has not been disputed. If a situation is minor, only about 4 percent of customers will speak up to someone who can help. When a problem is serious, around 23 percent will say something to someone who can help. That's about one in four, and it didn't include Janelle. As much as people think we are all complainers, we aren't.

LTIO: For this reason, we need to logically see every complaint we receive as a gift because complaints don't appear as often as problems occur. What would you have done if you had been in Janelle's situation?

You would think that after all the years humans have been complaining to each other that we would have learned how to handle them a bit better than letting them turn into major conflicts. Perhaps we would then learn to complain when it makes sense.

What if we looked at complaints as gifts?

Notes:

_____

_____

_____

_____

_____

_____

_____

_____

_____

_____

_____

_____

_____

_____

_____

_____

_____

_____

SELF-CHECK: Understanding Complaints

What are the three most important ideas you learned from chapter 2 about complaints?

1. _____

2. _____

3. _____

Why might so many people be reluctant to complain?

1. _____

2. _____

Maybe you ask for more feedback, but most CSRs don't ask for more complaints. This is because we know customers don't like to see themselves as complainers. But complaining isn't a bad word; it's a direct statement about expectations that haven't been met. How can we fix dissatisfaction if we don't hear about it? How do you distinguish the difference between feedback and complaints? Keep coming back to your definitions even if you prefer to call a complaint "feedback." It will help you differentiate the two terms and know what your customers are doing.

What is feedback? _____

_____

What are complaints? _____

_____

Who Complains?

Customers come in all sizes and shapes; they have different ethnicities, native languages, income levels, education, and social standing. Some are nice, while others are naturally hostile or arrogant.

Some are also like you!

When it comes to complainers, there are many different types as well. We'll look at four categories of complainers and use that information to better understand our customers.

Complainers Come in a Variety of Packages

In this chapter, we will look at four categories of people who complain. These categories aren't covered in the personality type studies you may have seen. We're going to look at their complaining behaviors. If you can recognize them, you will better know how to interact with them if they show up. One category is attempting to help you and is easy to recognize as they give you a "gift." The other three may never tell you they are upset—they just leave.

We are staying away from negative name-calling with these categories and instead focusing only on behaviors. One of these types of customers are the ones we want; the other three, not so much! Here are the four categories:

- The "I want you to get better" complainer
- The "I'm leaving" complainer
- The "online" complainer
- The "game the system" complainer

When encountering customers who complain, first listen to the content of the complaint they are presenting—not the way they are saying it. You'll have an easier time with complaint handling if you remember to do that. Remember, complainers arrive in a variety of packages.

Second, even if you never see them again as a customer, don't just wave goodbye. Ask why they are leaving you. Jewels of wisdom may be hidden in their answers. And sometimes, you can even turn them around to give you another chance to keep their business.

LTIO: When you meet a customer, in person or on the phone, how can you use the two pieces of advice on the previous page? You'll probably see that your answers become more complex the more you delve into this subject. You might want to come back to this page after you've completed more of the activities.

1. _____

2. _____

3. _____

Notes:

_____

_____

_____

_____

_____

_____

_____

_____

_____

_____

_____

_____

_____

_____

_____

_____

The "I Want You to Get Better" Complainer

We'd all love to only get compliments about our services and products, but that's not realistic. Sometimes we disappoint our customers, and they speak up.

At this point, we need to see who is talking with us. The people who want us to do better are our best customers because they are giving us a chance to improve so they don't leave us.

Even if they sound disappointed these complaining customers want you to improve, and if you do, they probably will stay with your business. That's good news! Generally, what these complainers say is accurate, even if it is specific to them. Their complaints may be fixable, providing you with usable information. It would be great if every customer were like this.

The complaint "The soup is too salty" is a perception that deals with taste buds. Since most customers do not complain, this customer may be acting as the spokesperson for other diners who also think the soup is too salty but won't say anything. This customer is alerting you about something you should look into.

You can guess this customer is asking about a detail that will determine whether they will return or not. If this customer regularly asks for this soup when they dine with you, they aren't likely to return unless you fix the excessive salty taste.

Even if this customer sounds a bit aggressive, they will still give you valuable information. Look beyond the "how" and listen to their "what." For example, if they say, with annoyance, "It's very difficult to reach anyone at your company; I called four times until someone answered the call!" Of course, they are annoyed, but they are still telling you they want you to improve. Listen to them!

LTIO: Over your next shift talking with customers, count on a slip of paper or on your phone the number of times you hear this type of complainer. Estimate the percentage of your customers who fall into this category: _____.

What have you learned from these "I want you to get better" customers about your company's business?

1. _____

2. _____

3. _____

LEARNING POINT: Customers who try to help you get better are giving you gifts. They are your partners in delivering your highest quality.

Notes:

_____

_____

_____

_____

_____

_____

_____

_____

_____

ACTIVITY

13

The "I'm Leaving" Complainer

Perhaps the most painful event for any CSR to handle is when a customer says, "I'm leaving and never coming back." You can feel their business slip through your fingers, and you don't know what to do.

It doesn't help to think, "Well, if that is what they want, then goodbye." Don't give up so easily. At a minimum, attempt to find out why they are leaving.

Some complainers have already decided to leave, no matter what you do. They mean it! Fed up with your company, they disagree with your practices or philosophy and probably have already found a better alternative. They believe they don't need you anymore, so in all likelihood, no matter how hard you try or what you do or say, they will leave.

However, you can still receive value from them by finding out why they are leaving. Getting them to talk might be difficult as they probably don't want to spend one more minute with you. Before they leave, you'll have to work hard to get the most information possible.

LTIO: Here are questions to consider:

1. What was the straw that broke that poor camel's back? Why are they leaving now? Why did they decide to use this last situation as the reason to leave you?
2. If they disagree with your practices or philosophy, what don't they like? If you ask them, they may say, for example, "You still use plastic when you could be using paper products." There's not much

you can do about that unless someone high up in the company decides to address this demand. But it's good information to have if there are hundreds more of these complaints.

3. If they are going to a competitor, why do they like them better? Is it pricing, service, or availability?

LEARNING POINT: Even if customers don't want to do business with you anymore, they can still give you highly valuable information.

Notes:

_____

_____

_____

_____

_____

_____

_____

_____

_____

_____

_____

_____

_____

_____

_____

The "Online" Complainer

Unfortunately, you can't always do something about online complainers. But that doesn't mean you shouldn't try.

If they leave negative feedback, treat it seriously and attempt to reach them personally. Reduce the amount of negative feedback by responding to them offline.

One key piece of advice is to not stoop to the same type of behavior they are using. As a CSR, you need to do what you can to protect your company's reputation.

Online complainers can post positive or negative comments. We are going to discuss only the malicious online complainers who post in an aggressive and deliberately poking manner, waiting for you to respond to the bait. These complainers seek to provoke, upset, and grab attention for themselves via inflammatory messages and even falsehoods. At times, these complainers are competitors who want to attack your reputation.

The problem is that many internet viewers will believe these complainers, leading to a loss of credibility—and customers.

Some companies do not allow comments to be made public on their websites until they have reviewed them. But online complainers know they can still make their comments public on other platforms. Unfortunately, negative comments get traction. You may hear comments from people who have read something posted by such a complainer. And who do those customers typically believe? That's why stopping these complainers early is crucial.

LTIO: Here's a video with some helpful ideas: www.ciag.online/14. Based on this video, how can you defend your company from these postings?

1. _____

2. _____

3. _____

LEARNING POINT: There are people in your company who watch for this type of internet activity. Your company's reputation is at stake, however. In your role, you are likely to hear about these attacks from other customers, so be sure to alert the people in your company who can do something to respond directly to these postings.

Notes:

_____

_____

_____

_____

_____

_____

_____

_____

_____

_____

_____

_____

15

The "Game the System" Complainer

Some complainers think if they complain, they will receive an advantage: a discount, a refund, a coupon, or another product or service. Some of these complainers purchase and then immediately complain to get a perk.

These customers challenge the system in a way that can be hard to detect unless your company has an extensive database that lets complaint handlers know about the frequency and type of complaint from each customer. Some companies offer thirty-day money-back guarantees. If you watch the return pattern, you might see a game-the-system customer return the product after twenty-nine days—and then repurchase the same product, only to bring it back again on day twenty-nine.

When complaining, some may ask, "What else will you give me?" which can offer a good clue as to what type of customer they are. If they don't get that extra discount or item, sometimes they threaten that they will speak badly about you and your company all over the internet.

Some of these customers are skillful at conducting fraud. Normally, they aren't attempting to game just your company; they are engaging in these activities against a number of others. Because it can represent significant revenue, most companies, especially large ones, put in controls in areas of potential exposure.

The fact that everyone needs to be alert is not pleasant. But as a CSR, you should know ways to identify and handle these complainers from your company. In this way, you can reduce these attacks.

If you have any questions that will help you discern what type of complainer is in front of you, be sure to raise them without attacking a customer who is perfectly innocent.

LTIO: Asking a few questions of someone in your department will provide guidance as to what you should do if you see this game being played. List whom to talk with and what you should do to stay in compliance with your company's policies.

1. Does your company's database help identify which customers show this pattern when they complain? Whom should you talk with, and what do they say?

_____

_____

2. What is the company policy about dealing with these customers? Most companies attempt to "fire" them, not letting them do business with you. Other companies treat these people as part of the cost of doing business and wave them through. As a CSR, what does your organization want you to do? Whom should you talk with, and what do they say?

_____

_____

LEARNING POINT: Even though there are people in the world who will attempt to game your system, it shouldn't change your belief in the essential honesty of most people. Maybe 4 percent game the system. Give your customers the benefit of the doubt. Don't assume they are all like the gamers. That would be a big mistake because it will impact how you treat everyone.

16

Who Is This Complainer?

We have just described four types of complainers:

- The "I want to help" complainer
- The "I'm leaving" complainer
- The "online" complainer
- The "game the system" complainer

LTIO: Can you identify them in action? To test yourself, go to: www .ciag.online/16. This video has four parts. Each person plays all four types of complainer. Write the type of complainer you see and why you think that person is that type. In the next activity, we will discuss the actions column. For now, please leave it blank.

Video	Type of Complainer	Characteristics	Actions
Part 1			
Part 2			
Part 3			
Part 4			

Was it easy to identify the type of complainer in each video? Could you tell right away? Or did you have to go back and consider all four before making a choice? It's okay if you did that, but when you are with a customer, you won't be able to.

Review your answers with a partner to see if you both agree on the type of complainer and their characteristics. For the correct answers, please go to www.ciag.online/16-b.

LEARNING POINT: Customers don't show up with labels on their foreheads. Sometimes, they change their behavior in the middle of interacting with a CSR. What do you do then? "Trust your judgment" is good advice!

Notes:

_____

_____

_____

_____

_____

_____

_____

_____

_____

_____

_____

_____

_____

_____

_____

Dealing with All Types of Complainers

Should you learn how to deal with all four types of complainers? Or should you primarily focus on the type who wants to help you get better? If you focus on the "I want to help" complainer, you'll probably get even more gifts from those customers. And that's valuable.

At the same time, if you learn to be flexible and deal with all four types, we also agree with you! You already know that you encounter many different types of complainers, and every customer can complain in different ways.

Have you ever been one of these four types of complainers? You probably have been the "I want to help" complainer. Perhaps the CSR helping you appreciated what you had to say. Have you been the "I'm leaving" complainer? Did you follow through on your threat? Have you ever tried to game a company's return policy? Why? Did you justify your behavior? Have you been a malicious internet complainer? What was the impact? Are you sure you want to do that again?

It's important to understand why we may have behaved in the same way. Then it becomes easier to understand our customers.

LTIO: Go to the actions column part of the table in Activity 16. Fill out possible actions you could use with each type of complainer. You can also find other options to deal with all four complainers at www .ciag.online/17.

LEARNING POINT: If we allow ourselves to be creative when responding to someone who has a complaint, we'll find our work more interesting. Human beings display enormous numbers of complaining behaviors. If all complainers were the same, it might get dull.

Responses for the Four Types of Complainers

Below are a series of responses you could use with the four types of complainers. Some of these actions could work with more than one type—or possibly with none.

LTIO: Beside each potential action, write the type of complainer for which you think this action would get the best results. Also indicate why this action would or would not work.

Use these abbreviations when you write the type of complainer.

- "I want to help" complainers: Helpers
- "I'm leaving" complainer: Leaving
- "Online" complainer: Online
- "Game the system" complainer: Gamer

Type	Response	Why this action would work or not
	Listen attentively	
	Interrupt and laugh	
	Ask, "If I had a magic wand, is there anything I can do to help you stay?"	

Type	Response	Why this action would work or not
	Ask, "Is there anything else we should improve?"	
	Thank them for their feedback.	
	Avoid answering to not encourage more of their behavior.	
	Set limits as to what you can do.	
	End with an action plan for what you will do for them.	
	Criticize the complainer.	
	Ask, "What should we do to keep you as a customer?"	
	Explain why you thank them.	

SELF-CHECK: Who Complains?

What are the three most important ideas you learned from chapter 3 about complainers?

1. _____

2. _____

3. _____

People often justify their behavior, especially when they are not all that proud of what they have done. How do online and game the system complainers justify their behavior? Does that help you understand them better?

Online: _____

Gamers: _____

We've identified four types of complainers. Of course, there are more than four types. Let your imagination go, and name and describe other types of complainers. Don't make them all negative complainers. Think of a mix of different types of complainers, some we might consider positive for our business. If you share these ideas with others, you probably will become quite good at picking out other types. Remember, complainers come in all different types. The better we recognize and identify them, the better we'll know how to effectively deal with them.

1. _____

2. _____

3. _____

CHAPTER 4

The Treasure of
Complaints as Gifts

The true treasure of complaints is that if handled well, customers often feel more positively toward an organization than if they didn't encounter a problem in the first place. We also learn from our customers when they complain.

If these are the outcomes resulting from complaints, why wouldn't we look for more customer feedback or complaints? Yet many companies seek to eliminate this treasure trove.

In this chapter, we will look at five reasons why complaints are gifts.

How Your Emotions Affect Your Complaint Handling

We say complaints are gifts, but are they?

LTIO: Circle the negative emotions that come to mind when you hear "I have a complaint."

Ambivalence	Disbelief	Guilt	Insecurity
Anger	Discomfort	Hatred	Panic
Animosity	Disgust	Helplessness	Rage
Annoyance	Dislike	Hostility	Resentment
Defensiveness	Distrust	Inadequacy	Sadness

Choose two of these emotions, and write how holding these negative emotions could impact your complaint handling.

Negative emotion: _____

Impact: _____

Negative emotion: _____

Impact: _____

What would be your reaction if we listed positive feelings instead of negative emotions? Circle all the positive emotions you think of when you hear "I have a complaint."

Amusement	Care	Happiness	Lightheartedness
Anticipation	Curiosity	High energy	Motivation
Appreciation	Excitement	Hope	Pride
Awe	Generosity	Inspiration	Selflessness
Calm	Gratitude	Interest	Surprise

Now choose two of these emotions, and write how if you held these positive emotions they would impact your complaint handling.

Positive emotion:_____

Impact: _____

Positive emotion:_____

Impact: _____

LEARNING POINT: Our emotional state will impact how we react to complaints, so fostering positive emotions is a good idea.

Finding the positive is not always easy. Sometimes complaints are gifts that come wrapped in ugly paper with thorns and needles attached. But the important thing is to look beyond the outer appearance and find the learning that will help us improve.

Notes:

_____

_____

_____

_____

_____

_____

_____

Five Reasons Why Complaints Are Gifts

When we first began to explore the A Complaint Is a Gift concept, we primarily focused on two advantages of this philosophy. First, complaints are the biggest bargain in market research. Complaints tell us what our customers like and don't like. The second advantage involves customer loyalty—if you handle customers' complaints well, they tend to stick with you.

Then about ten years later, we added to the list of advantages and are now at five reasons why complaints are gifts. Complaints are gifts because they

- Define what customers want
- Help identify the most loyal customers
- Are the least expensive marketing tool around
- Mean that customers are still talking with us and not anyone else
- Help retain customers if their complaints are handled well

LTIO: Think about these reasons. Could they change your approach to complaints if you think they are advantageous?

_____

_____

_____

Come back to each of these reasons as you progress through this chapter. They are essential in your mindset development to see complaints as gifts.

For instance, imagine that a complaining customer is standing in front of you, and these five advantages pass through your mind. They can help you avoid assuming that a grouchy customer doesn't appreciate what you do to solve their problems. What would be your attitude instead? How would your attitude about your customer change?

Notes:

_____

_____

_____

_____

_____

_____

_____

_____

_____

_____

_____

_____

_____

_____

Complaints Define What Customers Want

Have you ever had a good idea for a business when you were a customer? Maybe you said, "Hey, why don't you . . ."

Here's an example. Janelle bought an expensive coffee maker that she loves. Unfortunately, after a couple of months, the glass carafe that collects the brewed coffee broke. The glass was fragile, and it shattered while she was cleaning it.

Because the carafe is probably the least expensive part of the coffee maker, Janelle thought she could easily replace it on Amazon.

Not possible. Of course, the manufacturer makes the carafes, or they wouldn't have them to provide with the coffee maker! But neither Amazon nor the manufacturer sells replacement carafes.

Then Janelle noticed that she wasn't the only one with the same problem. Dozens of people had the same issue. They didn't blame the manufacturer or Amazon. They just wanted to buy a replacement for the shattered carafes.

LTIO: Imagine you are the CSR who handles complaints about the carafes. A customer calls with the same problem Janelle experienced. Everyone in your company knows about this recurring problem, including you. After all, it's in all the comments online. Everyone is rating your coffee maker very low as a result of no carafe replacements.

What do you say to these customers? You don't know for sure that your company will start to sell the carafes as replacement items, but it's what customers want. Write your ideas on the lines below.

_____

_____

_____

Tell a partner what you would say and ask if your response would satisfy them. If they don't like what you said, ask what it would take to make them happy. Write their comments here.

_____

_____

_____

Based on your partners' comments, what would you say to customers who call? Write it here and check back with your partner to see if your adjustment would work for them.

_____

_____

_____

When you learn about a similar product or service issue from your customers, consider who you should tell inside your company.

ACTIVITY

22

Complaints Tell Us Who Is Loyal

Forbes Councils is an invitation-only organization that gains solid advice from its business members. Here's such an example from one of its members: "I find that it is often a business's most loyal customers who are more likely to complain in the first place. These individuals are already displaying a certain level of brand affinity to care enough to actually take the time to get in touch."[1]

Does this match you? When you complain, are you a more loyal customer?

LTIO: Think of an example when you intensely disliked a service or product. You feel you got a rotten deal the first time you bought something from a company. After the second time you purchased from it and are again disappointed, you are never going back.

How likely are you to complain? Circle a number.

1   2   3   4   5   6   7   8   9   10
Not likely   Highly likely

Let's change the scenario a little. You shop at a company you have been going to for at least a few years. You like the people who work there, and you like the brand and its products and services. But you had a problem the last time you shopped there.

Are you likely to go to the trouble to complain? Circle a number.

1   2   3   4   5   6   7   8   9   10

Not likely   Highly likely

What would you expect from this company or brand?

_____

_____

When a complaining customer approaches you, do you think it would be a good idea to assume that this person is likely a loyal customer? Imagine a sticky note on their forehead with a number indicating the years they've been loyal or how much money they have spent with you. This figure can indicate how valuable this customer is to you.

Notes:

_____

_____

_____

_____

_____

_____

_____

_____

_____

_____

_____

Complaints Are an Inexpensive Marketing Tool

Companies spend an enormous part of their budgets learning about their customers and marketing to them. They use various tools, including focus groups, reviews of consumer expectations in parallel industries, transaction-based studies, and mystery shoppers. If you're not in marketing or you don't recognize these terms, don't worry.

The important thing for you to know is that your complaint handling is much more dynamic and happens in real time. Large companies use tools like those listed above, which are necessary. But small and medium-sized companies must rely on customers to tell them directly what they think. None of the tools listed above bring customers closer to you than complaint handling. Customers will likely have something specific to say if they are asked while complaining. These gifts are useful because they occur in real-life situations.

There is an old example that makes this point. In the mid-1980s, Coca-Cola conducted research on its New Coke concept. But people blasted Coke with complaints on its eight hundred phone lines when the new product was released in place of the now Coke Classic. They protested at Coke's Atlanta headquarters and threatened never to buy Coke again. Even though the new concept had passed with flying colors in survey and tasting research, customers felt betrayed. Without question, marketing research is valuable, but nothing compares to having your fingers on the pulse of customer preferences.

LTIO: Ask someone in your marketing department if they ever listen to customer complaints. Why or why not? If they say they listen closely in focus groups, that's not the same. How do they see complaint handling as part of their toolbox?

_____

_____

_____

_____

_____

_____

_____

Notes:

_____

_____

_____

_____

_____

_____

_____

_____

_____

_____

_____

Complainers Are Still Talking with You

Have you ever been in a conflict where you or another person were so upset with each other that you stopped talking for a while? It could have been over something like forgetting to stop by the grocery store on the way home from work to pick up a container of milk or forgetting that yesterday was your birthday.

What happened next?

We've talked with people who won't say another word to someone they've been close to—sometimes not speaking for years. If no talking occurs for a lengthy time, it probably means the relationship is over. If this happens between family members, family gatherings can get awkward when adult siblings or parents and children don't talk with each other.

How about the opposite? You and a family member rarely talk with each other without getting snippy or irritated. Which situation is better: not talking or getting annoyed while talking? The choice is up to you, of course.

Eventually, people have to communicate with each other, or whatever relationship they have will end, so maybe some talking is good. Let's apply this principle to customers.

If our customers stop talking with us, what's going to happen to that relationship? If customers don't tell you what's bothering them, they are probably telling others. If that's the case, do you think they are saying nice things about you? Likely not. Who would you prefer they talk to about their complaints, you or the marketplace?

The choice is up to us. Be open to listening. Keep asking for customer feedback, even if the customer is sarcastic and hostile.

LEARNING POINT: If a customer is upset with you while complaining, at least they are still talking with you. Celebrate that!

Notes:

_____

_____

_____

_____

_____

_____

_____

_____

_____

_____

_____

_____

_____

_____

_____

_____

_____

ACTIVITY

25

Complaints Are an Opportunity to Keep Your Customers

What are your customer-retention numbers? Ask someone in marketing or customer service to help you answer the questions below.

How many customers does your company lose every year because of poor service or product quality? What does that mean in terms of revenue lost every year? An estimate will do. How many new customers does your business (or department) have to get each year just to replace the ones the business loses?

_____

These numbers are important and can represent a significant amount of money lost to businesses each year.

Have you ever had a negative service or product experience that you now remember as positive? Researchers have found that close to 25 percent of customers surveyed stated that all positive memories of incidents from airline, hotel, and restaurant industries started as service delivery failures. Yet they remained loyal customers.[2] The numbers might differ for companies that sell high-ticket items, but this research still makes a compelling point.

LTIO: Think of an example of a personal negative event that ended up being positive for you. What happened? What do you think about it now? What did the complaint handler do to turn your assessment of the incident into something positive?

_____

How to Get More Complaints

We've listed five reasons why complaints are gifts. Perhaps we should get more complaints. We think that's a good idea.

You should encourage more customers to speak up and tell you how to do something better. Even if you don't implement all their suggestions, these customers are engaged, feel connected to you, and are signaling they would like your company to get better.

LTIO: How can you get more complaints? Share your ideas below.

1. _____

_____

2. _____

_____

3. _____

_____

4. _____

_____

5. _____

_____

Ask your customers directly under which circumstances they would comfortably give you more feedback. You can tell them you are doing this for a workshop you are taking. They'll probably help!

1. _____

_____

2. _____

_____

3. _____

_____

4. _____

_____

5. _____

_____

Here are four more ideas we think will work to get additional customer feedback.

1. Use every opportunity to ask your customers what they think (e.g., about your products, service, pricing). By requesting that customers provide their opinions, you create a psychological contract with them that says, "I value you, and I want to know as much as I can how to help you." It's like shaking someone's hand on an agreement.
2. We'll say this several times in this workbook: show your customers you take their opinions seriously by writing their comments down. Serious listening sends the message that you value them—especially if you ask how they think you can improve.

3. After a customer shares feedback, be sure to ask, "Is there anything more?" which shows you're not afraid of their feedback or complaints.

4. If you get a good idea you can use, be sure to tell them how much you appreciate their input. Of course, you can't just say those words. You've got to believe it.

LTIO: The next time you talk with a customer, try one—or all four—of these ideas and see if they grace you with an additional gift! What happened with each of these ideas?

Idea 1. _____

Idea 2. _____

Idea 3. _____

Idea 4. _____

Notes:

_____

_____

_____

_____

_____

_____

_____

_____

_____

_____

When Organizations Stop Getting Complaints

The bankruptcy of major companies is painful for large numbers of staff, customers, and shareholders. The loss of Pan American Airways was a business tragedy. It called itself the "World's Most Experienced Airline," while other people called it the "World's Most Arrogant Airline."

The airline existed for sixty-four years and was once the world's largest international carrier. It was a jewel among airlines. It set world records and launched the Boeing 747 airplane, which was primarily used for international travel as the aircraft never worked for Pan Am in the US domestic market. High fuel costs that had not been adequately anticipated and managed was a big part of its problem. In January 1991, Pan Am was sold to United Airlines in bankruptcy proceedings.

The Pan Am brand was so strong that it still lives on. Other airlines have attempted to use the name and soar in the skies once again. None succeeded. Nonetheless, the name is a legacy and one of the most prominently branded names in aviation history.

At the company's end, regular mishaps were experienced, and it lost $5 million per day. Passengers were fed up with Pan Am's inability to fix customer issues, so people stopped flying with the airline.

In a letter to a major newspaper editor right before Pan Am was sold to United Airlines, a staff member wrote that service had gotten so bad that customers stopped complaining. They knew it wouldn't do any good. The letter talked about a chartered Pan Am 747 jet filled with a group going on a weeklong all-inclusive vacation. The plane arrived at the resort a day late with none of the passengers' luggage.

According to the frustrated employee, not a single passenger complained.

Janelle flew Pan Am internationally in its last year of operation. Her experience was that it did not live up to its reputation either. Lack of motivation to serve customers was noticeable. Though it was once considered prestigious to fly Pan Am, the flight didn't match the hype. Both passengers and crew were unmotivated.

LEARNING POINT: Even a great reputation won't help if service or products aren't delivered. If no improvements are made to keep once-loyal customers, they will give up and stop complaining regardless of how well-known the business is.

LTIO: Think of any current well-branded business that you suspect may not last for the long haul. What have you noticed happening that makes you think that way? It tells us how important complaint handling is.

_____

_____

Notes:

_____

_____

_____

_____

_____

_____

_____

SELF-CHECK: The Treasure of Complaints as Gifts

Which do you think is the most important of the five reasons why complaints are gifts? Why is it the most important reason for your company?

_____

_____

What questions should you ask to learn more about what your customers want when you hear them talking about something that dissatisfied them?

_____

_____

What questions should you ask of long-term complaining customers to learn why they want to leave your company, or what it would take to get them to stay?

_____

_____

What should you say to customers who indicate they are thinking about not returning? What types of statements will perhaps encourage them to give your organization another chance?

_____

_____

CHAPTER 5

The Gift Formula

Victoria says it so well: "Complaints are like oysters: they might not be pretty on the outside, but inside you will find a beautiful gift—a valuable pearl."

A Complaint Is a Gift is a compelling title. It's not what we generally expect when we see or hear a complaint heading our direction. However, there is value in customer comments, especially when customers are dissatisfied. We call this value a gift.

We've looked at understanding complaints, learned about who complains, and examined why complaints are gifts. Next, we'll discover how to find those gifts and get more of them. We'll start with the Gift Formula, a go-to response when you hear a complaint.

Complaints as Birthday Gifts

Let's clear things up. The gifts within customer complaints are not like a birthday present. They're a metaphor. Frankly, we're disappointed, or ought to be, when we hear a complaint because it means that we disappointed a customer. Sometimes, these complaints are difficult to fix. Why do we then offer a Gift Formula that reinforces the idea that a complaint is a gift? The gift is the communication with customers that will help fix their issue and turn them into satisfied—and maybe even happy—customers.

When complaints are made, your mindset about complaints has a significant influence on what will happen. It probably helps more than just about anything else you can do when handling complaints. Instead of rushing to judgment, such as "Why can't these customers talk a little faster?" or "How many times do I have to explain this to them?" you will see the gift that is being offered to you. If you see the complaint as an opportunity—as a gift—it helps.

You need to develop and nurture this mindset. It's helpful if your teammates talk the language of complaint giving as gifts. Adopting this mindset will be easier if this idea is reinforced at every meeting, on wall posters, and in all conversations and training sessions about customer service.

LTIO: List one specific thing you can do to reinforce your mindset about seeing complaints as gifts.

_____

_____

How can you reinforce the mindset that a complaint is a gift in the minds of all the people you work with? List three ways.

_____

_____

_____

You can also strengthen the mindset that complaints are gifts by personally reinforcing any of your company's policies, operational systems, communication systems, mission, vision, and values that support a complaint-friendly philosophy. List what you can do to reinforce your company's efforts to bolster the idea of complaints as gifts.

_____

_____

_____

LEARNING POINT: When it comes to accepting a complaint as a gift, your mindset matters!

Notes:

_____

_____

_____

_____

_____

_____

_____

_____

What Is the Gift Formula?

Imagine a good friend gives you a lovely wrapped gift to celebrate your birthday. Everything about you would show how pleased you are to receive their present. After saying hello, you would immediately thank them. "Wow! Thank you. Thank you for remembering my birthday. You know, you didn't need to bring me a gift."

What if you opened the gift and found a box of candy—chocolates, your favorite! What would you say? "Wow! Thank you. I'm so pleased. I haven't had these candies for months! How thoughtful of you. I'll think of you as I eat each one. In fact, why don't we both take one right now!"

Okay, maybe you wouldn't say exactly that, but something along those lines.

Now imagine you work in a call center handling issues about cell phones. A customer calls with a complaint: "My name is Sam Johnson, and I can't get decent reception on my new phone. I keep getting disconnected, and yet your advertising goes on and on about how you've got the most reliable network around. And that's not all. But that doesn't surprise me." Would you say, "Thank you for calling and telling us about this. How thoughtful of you. I appreciate it"? Probably not.

But when we receive a birthday present, we do not hesitate to say, "Thank you." Why do we do this?

We thank our friend because they took the time to get us something we would like. What about complaining customers? Are they friends or enemies? What are most of them trying to do?

It's as if they have gifted us with a box of chocolates named, "Listen to Me, Treat Me Well, and I'll Continue to Be Your Customer."

You don't want to respond with "Go away. I already ate a box like this last month. I'm on a diet, and I don't want to eat anymore. I'm already too heavy."

When encountering a complaint about products or services, many CSRs will start by asking a barrage of identification questions: "What is your name? How do you spell that? What's your phone number? Is that your cell phone? What's your email? What's your address? When did you start your service? What is the product number of your phone? (By the way, it's on the bottom of the box in which it came in such tiny digits you'll need a magnifying glass to read it.) Do you have your monthly bill in front of you? And when did you send in your last payment?"

Telephone company CSRs may blame the weather, sighing and saying, "We hear a lot of complaints about this, but it's due to the high winds we've been having." They may attack their own company by saying, "Those dropped calls on cell phones happen a lot, but we're dealing with a lot of issues that we have no control over."

If customers are fortunate, they will get an apology. But few customer service people will say, "Thank you," right off the bat.

Have you ever complained and heard "Thank you" from the CSR immediately? Probably not. It's extremely rare. If you ever hear "Thank you" right after you complain, check in with yourself to see how you feel.

Some complaint handlers may say "Thank you" at the end of the conversation, by which time customers are likely so annoyed, it's a meaningless phrase.

Most people think it would be wonderful to live in a world where every complaint is received as a gift. But mostly complaint handlers think customers should change and become the gracious ones.

What if we could learn to be gracious to customers—not only the ones who are purchasing but also the ones who complain about those purchases? What if we could learn to accept feedback from friends, colleagues, and family graciously? Let's not wait for everyone else to change. Let's change ourselves first.

LTIO: What do you do when you get a gift you don't want? What do you say? What might you be thinking?

_____

_____

_____

Notes:

_____

_____

_____

_____

_____

_____

_____

_____

_____

_____

_____

The Gift Formula Overview

The Gift Formula is organized into a series of steps so you always know where you are in the process. Having said this, you may find occasions when it is more appropriate to vary the sequence or enhance the suggested phrases with your own equivalent language. But the most robust way to begin is with a simple "Thank you."

You can also combine the steps. We've heard some good combination of phrases. When you first use the Gift Formula, try to follow it as written here. But our intention is not to give you a script but rather to provide guidelines.

The Gift Formula is broken down into three main steps, some with their own substeps.

1. Respond by building rapport.
   a. Say, "Thank you."
   b. Briefly explain why you are happy your customer spoke up.
   c. Apologize briefly but sincerely.
   d. Tell your customer what you will do.
2. Recover by fixing the issue.
   a. Ask for information.
   b. Fix the issue as quickly as you can.
   c. Follow up to check for satisfaction.
3. Address the issue inside the organization so it doesn't recur.

If you are acquainted with the first or second edition of *A Complaint Is a Gift*, you may recall there were eight steps. When we worked with a large cruise line where most of the crew's mother tongue was not English, we found it was easier for them to remember three steps. As a result, we grouped the eight steps into three. Everything is still there. It's just easier to remember with three steps.

LTIO: To remember what you need to do to treat a complaint as a gift, repeat the three steps with their subsets until you can say them from memory.

Notes:

_____

_____

_____

_____

_____

_____

_____

_____

_____

_____

_____

_____

_____

_____

_____

Respond by Saying "Thank You"

Rapport is a French word that means to create a relationship where people understand each other. When you have rapport, you get along and cooperate.

Rapport is great to share when you handle a complaint. You'll especially want to create this feeling when your customer arrives in a bad mood. Under those circumstances, the quicker you can build rapport, the better for both of you.

If you have a good rapport with your colleagues or neighbors, it doesn't matter if you make a small mistake. You fix it, and they don't attack you. The same is true when it comes to customer complaints. Customers will likely share their complaints without hostility if you start with rapport because they know you intend to help them.

People who are in rapport are usually open, tolerant, and cooperative. They feel confident in how you will take care of them, which is not a bad place to start when handling a complaint. The four substeps of this Gift Formula item will move you toward a relationship of rapport. The four substeps of this Gift Formula item include the following:

- Say, "Thank you."
- Briefly explain why you are happy your customer spoke up.
- Apologize briefly but sincerely.
- Tell your customer what you will do.

These four short, simple steps, which are all about building rapport, will move you toward a good starting point for handling your customer's complaint.

Remember, you are receiving a gift. What do you say when receiving a gift, even if you don't want it? You say, "thank you."

We know it feels a little uncomfortable to start with saying "Thank you," especially if the customer doesn't look happy.

But the customer isn't expecting to hear "Thank you." It startles them. Often, they will get a surprised look on their face, and then they are likely to say, "You're welcome." After all, people are expected to say, "You're welcome," after they hear "Thank you."

In almost all languages, "Thank you" is followed by some form of "You're welcome." It's built into our communication exchanges. We've lost count of how many people have told us how angry complaining customers settle down when they hear "Thank you."

LTIO: The next time you hear someone share a complaint, give them a chance to complete their sentence. But as soon as they pause, say "Thank you." Just try that much. We'll show you what to do in the next activity. Watch the video of Janelle demonstrating the Gift Formula at www.ciag.online/31.

Notes:

_____

_____

_____

_____

_____

_____

_____

_____

_____

ACTIVITY

32

Build Stronger Rapport

Building rapport isn't difficult to do. People engage in rapport-building activities all the time when they want to maintain a sense of harmony and goodwill.

As a CSR, don't just wait for the customer to build rapport with you. Take the first step yourself.

LTIO: Rapport can be strengthened in a number of ways. List four ways that can help you and your customer enter into a supportive relationship. We've started the list with smiling, which is the easiest way to begin building rapport. Someone who is smiling looks like they have your best interests at heart. It disarms people when they are upset.

1.   Smile at your customer.

2.   _____

3.   _____

4.   _____

Saying "Thank you" is also a good way to begin the process of creating rapport. Even though it's not enough to take care of a complaint, it builds the foundation for establishing a relationship where that can happen.

When you fix a customer's problem, you take the customer to the emotional space where they felt good—when they first made their purchase. But to keep them as a long-term customer, you need to move them beyond that original good feeling and help them feel better. Showing your gratitude helps.

You need to say what hearing the complaint means to you and why you appreciate the feedback. "Thank you" by itself can sound cynical or scripted.

For example, the information they are sharing with you will allow you to better fix the problem or change something in your service processes to make sure others won't face the same issue. You can say, "Thank you for speaking up," "Thank you, I'm really glad you told me so I can fix this for you," or simply, "We're better than this. Thanks for letting me know."

Your complete thought needs to go something like this: "Thank you for telling me about this problem. You can't imagine how many customers just walk away without saying anything, even though they're really dissatisfied, and we probably lose their business. They then tell other people without giving us the opportunity to make things right. And we definitely want to keep your business. That way we can be better at giving our customers what they want. That's why we really do appreciate your taking the time and trouble to come up to us and say something. Thank you, thank you, from the bottom of my heart."

That's the complete mindset, but don't say all of that. You'd probably scare customers away. But you can think it.

Then you need to apologize like you mean it. And finally, tell them you are going to take care of their problem. Wouldn't you like to hear that?

LEARNING POINT: Remember, you aren't just fixing a problem for your customers. You need to address their emotions and help them feel satisfied so they want to return.

Apologies Matter

A recent national customer rage study asked customers what they wanted when they complained: 75 percent said an apology, but only 28 percent receive one.[1]

When customers complain, they may not hear an apology even if one is given. If a customer doesn't hear your apology, you might as well not have given one. They were probably so involved in complaining they didn't hear it. That's why it's a good idea when writing a response to a complaint to apologize close to the start of your response and then apologize again at the conclusion.

Be careful not to overapologize. One business school studied apologies and found at call centers that CSRs who inspired the most confidence did apologize. But then they didn't repeat those apologies. They said it once or twice when handling a call, but then they stopped saying it. It becomes burdensome to the customer. Customers feel compelled to say something in response to the apology, such as "Never mind, that's okay." The customers can begin to feel they are taking care of the CSR instead of vice versa.[2]

Many organizations tell their employees to apologize first. Is this your company's approach? We think there is a better way.

LTIO: If you have been told to start your complaint handling with an apology, ask someone in your organization why that decision was made. You can tell them that this program you are completing recommends a better way—that is, say "Thank you."

Beginning with a "Thank you" starts a chain of effective communication both the speaker and listener can exchange. When we hear "Thank you," it makes us think someone will do something for us.

When we hear, "I'm sorry," it leaves us feeling that is all we are going to get—and that's why the person is apologizing.

You can give an apology, but don't start with "I'm sorry." Wait until you have created rapport.

LTIO: What does an apology mean to you? When you hear someone say, "I'm sorry," what impact does it have on you? List three positive reactions you have when hearing an apology.

1. _____

2. _____

3. _____

Does saying "I'm sorry" have any negative consequences? What we say affects our customers, so we need to understand both the positive and negative sides of these words. List three negative reactions you have when hearing an apology.

1. _____

2. _____

3. _____

LEARNING POINT: An apology isn't just a bunch of words. It means something special. For many customers, it's the most important thing they receive when complaining. But it can be overdone.

The Power of Apologies

Apologies involve a special kind of sharing. They make it easier for customers to forgive service or product problems.

For some of our customers to continue doing business with us, they need to forgive us. This requires that they hear an apology. People often struggle to let go of the past without forgiveness.

Social psychologists have said that forgiving is one of the most fundamental processes that keeps relationships strong.[3] If our customers don't forgive us for something we did to them because they never heard an apology, they won't be sure if they want to come back to us. Or if they do return, they are likely to walk in with a chip on their shoulders. It will be easy to offend them again, and we'll never know why they are upset.

Many CSRs assume the customer is just an unpleasant person in situations like this. They probably don't consider that this customer may be carrying old baggage. They never received an apology from us—or our colleagues—for something.

LTIO: How easy is it for you to provide a sincere apology? This doesn't mean saying a quick "Sorry" but instead offering a sincere apology that our customer or someone else can hear. Circle one option below to describe how hard or easy it is for you to apologize to someone.

Easy	Not so easy	Difficult

What Do Apologies Mean to Me?

Some people think that if they apologize that means they are responsible for what happened. They may recognize that their customers would like an apology, but when CSRs are listening to a specific complaint, such as, "This item broke before I even got it home," they are thinking, "Why should I have to apologize? I wasn't even there."

LTIO: Instead of reacting defensively, what could you say to yourself? For example, you could instead think, "It really doesn't matter that I wasn't there. The customer felt the impact. I can apologize about that." How could you respond in the following situations?

- Instead of "I didn't make that mistake. It was my colleague," I could say:

  _____

- Instead of "Why should I apologize? They were so nasty to me," I could say:

  _____

- Instead of "Just a simple mistake. No need for an apology," I could say:

  _____

When service providers demonstrate their concern for their customers with apologies, exchanged empathy becomes a part of the communication process.

The wonderful aspect about apologies is that most people will tell you things are okay once they hear the magic words, "I'm sorry." Most customers will respond, "Look, it's really okay. I know you didn't do it yourself. It's just the system, but I appreciate your apology."

But you've got to mean the words. There's nothing worse than a faked, forced "I'm sorry."

In the complaint-handling business, if you don't feel your apologies or emphathize with your customers, you are better off not using the powerful words, "I'm sorry. Please let me apologize."

Notes:

_____

_____

_____

_____

_____

_____

_____

_____

_____

_____

_____

_____

ACTIVITY

36

Now Fix It!

At this point in the complaint-handling process, you need something from the customer. You've quickly established rapport so the customer knows you will follow through and do something for them. But you need more information: "For me to help you, could you please give me some information?"

Don't say, "I need some information; otherwise, I can't help you." You're now the one asking for help. The customer brought you a gift. You've thanked them, told them why you're grateful, apologized, and said you would help them.

Get as much information as you need. Make sure you ask for enough, or you'll have to come back for more. Sometimes when you ask for information, you learn what's truly bothering your customers. They may have said one thing, believing they have accurately presented the problem, but after asking a few questions, you both may discover the issue is different. At this step, a genuine problem-solving discussion can take place.

When you fix the customer's complaint, do it as quickly as possible. Speed means a lot to customers. You should give them as much information about what happened as they need.

LTIO: After fixing a problem at your next customer interaction, ask "Are you satisfied? Have we taken care of everything? Is there anything else we can do?" What type of responses did your customer make after you asked the above questions?

37

Your Company Needs to Make It Right

Wouldn't it be great if you didn't have to keep hearing about the same problems over and over again?

After you've established rapport with your customers and fixed specific problems, you and your organization need to learn something from these experiences. After all, you don't want to keep hearing the same complaints, so it's time to manage them. You were handling them by creating rapport and fixing problems. Now you need to manage the complaints to prevent them from happening again in the future.

How did this problem happen? You probably have some idea what needs to happen after talking with customers. No doubt people were involved in the issue, but what types of processes generated the mistake?

The root causes of the problem must be identified for the complaint to truly become a gift. As a Hewlett-Packard executive in the customer-satisfaction department located in Cupertino, California, once said, "We can say we're listening, but it's not until we take action that things really start happening."[4]

Don't just fix problems for the customer you helped. Correct these issues for all customers as well as your entire company. If you've got an idea, share it with your manager. Become the fixer who discovers the revenue that comes from correcting problems.

LTIO: List the three most common complaints you receive. Check to see if your coworkers agree with you about your choice.

1. _____

2. _____

3. _____

ACTIVITY

38

Say It Like You Mean It

Why is saying "Thank you" so magical? Many studies report that showing gratitude produces neurotransmitters in the brain, which makes us feel good. This occurs in both the grateful person and the receiver as well.[5]

For this release of hormones to occur, the "Thank you" must sound sincere. Are you sincere when you apologize?

LTIO: Go to www.ciag.online/38. Mark each audio on the chart below with whether the speaker's "Thank you" sounds genuine or fake. Describe what makes you believe it's genuine or fake.

Situation	Genuine or fake	Comments

LTIO: Ask for direct feedback from two colleagues and two family members after you use the Gift Formula. Ask if you sounded sincere when you said "Thank you." If you didn't, ask them why. Use them as your coach until you can say these two simple words from your heart.

People who gave me feedback	Comments
At work	
At work	
At home	
At home	

Notes:

_____

_____

_____

_____

_____

_____

_____

_____

_____

_____

_____

_____

_____

_____

_____

_____

Follow Up with Customers

When you follow each step of the Gift Formula, you are participating more fully in your company's business. You are learning that to succeed in business, you need to satisfy your customers. Whatever you end up doing throughout your life, you'll succeed by continuing to act on this statement.

LTIO: Choose a customer you have helped with their complaint. You'll need their email address or their telephone number to do this. Perhaps give them a heads up that you will contact them to make sure their issue was handled.

Call or send them an email saying that you are checking in with them to see if everything is okay. They'll probably fall out of their chairs if you do this. If the problem persists, you can help them again, and you will have a very grateful customer. You will have come full circle, and likely they will say "Thank you" to you.

Notes:

_____

_____

_____

_____

_____

_____

Victoria's "Thank You" Story

Victoria learned the Gift Formula more than twenty-five years ago. She taught these concepts and practiced them in real life every time she heard a complaint. She was so committed to the strength of the Gift Formula, she would teach her students the concept and then check in to see if they still used the formula—even weeks, months, or years after they took the seminar.

In March 1998, the Gift Formula became Victoria's most valuable lesson learned. She was at home, seven months pregnant, while her husband, Tom, had dinner with friends. Around midnight, Tom called to say he was coming home. A short while later, in a terrified voice, he called to say, "Call the police, I've been kidnapped! Call—" Victoria could hear a man asking who he was talking to. Imagine being in such a situation!

Victoria was desperate. A minute later, she got another call, this time from the kidnapper himself. In a menacing, aggressive voice, he said, "I have your husband, and I'm going to kill him if you don't give me a million pesos *now!* You understand?" What would you have said?

Victoria didn't even think about it. After using the Gift Formula so many times, it was now in her unconscious brain. The first words she said were "Thank you! Thank you. I know you will be a good man and take care of him. I'll give you all I have, everything, just please take care of him. You see, he's going to be a father in a few days." Silence followed.

Victoria imagines that he must have been confused. Tom told her later that the kidnapper, laughing, told the others, "This woman is nuts!" He certainly didn't expect her response.

In a much less aggressive voice, he asked Victoria, "Okay, what do you have?" She described all that she had, including jewelry and cash. He said, "It's not much, but okay. I will meet you at X location at 2 a.m." And then he added, "If you call the police, I will shoot your husband. If you call anyone, even your family, I will kill him. If you are not on time and bring all you said you have, I will shoot him. I will be monitoring you. And if you don't show up alone, I'll shoot him in front of you."

"Don't worry, I'll bring all I have. Just please don't hurt him. I know he's in your good hands, and you'll be kind to him. Thank you. I'm sure your mother raised you to be a good man. Are you a father?" He grumbled and hung up.

Victoria started loading everything in her car—money, jewelry, VCRs, CDs, and even a microwave—a heavy load for a pregnant woman!

At 2 a.m., she got to where he told her to be. She was alone, and her car was loaded on a deserted street in a dangerous part of the city. She waited, and waited, and waited. 2:30 a.m. 3 a.m. 3:30 a.m. Nothing.

Victoria thought they had probably killed her husband and that they wouldn't show up. She was scared and crying. Every possibility went through her mind. Finally, she got a phone call.

It was her husband. He was alive! He said that after the kidnappers spoke to her, they changed their minds. They stopped punching him. They put him in the trunk of the car, drove far away, and then left him—beaten and with no money or mobile phone, but alive. They kept telling him, "Keep the blinders on until we leave." He did that and then walked miles until he found a phone to call Victoria.

This never happens with kidnappers! Whatever Victoria had said to the primary kidnapper must have completely shook him. To this day, every time Tom meets Janelle, he thanks the Gift Formula and her for saving his life.

LTIO: We know this story sounds almost too good to be true, but it really did happen. Write down your reaction and what you learned from reading about Victoria's experience.

_____

_____

_____

Notes:

_____

_____

_____

_____

_____

_____

_____

_____

_____

_____

_____

_____

_____

_____

_____

ACTIVITY

41

Practicing the Gift Formula

We have both learned it takes practice to feel at ease and start by say-ing "Thank you" when hearing a complaint. This means practicing the Gift Formula in nonchallenging situations—such as with colleagues, friends, and family.

LTIO: Set up practice sessions with someone who is also going through these materials. We've listed several complaints below. Because they are so varied, most will not hit the mark precisely for you. But that's okay because you are practicing.

After you read why this customer is complaining, practice going through just the first step of the Gift Formula to build rapport. You don't need to go through the second or third steps.

1. A customer has called to say his order promised for delivery two days ago still hasn't arrived. He really needs this item, but he is more upset about your company not keeping its word.
2. A customer walks up to you in a retail store and doesn't know what to do. She has been waiting for more than a half hour and has to leave to pick up her child. The customer doesn't know what to do as she feels she has waited too long to just leave. Can you help?
3. You work as a host in an upscale restaurant. A couple walks in expecting to be immediately seated because they have a reservation—or at least they thought they did. They are upset. They can see that someone is at their favorite table that they usually get. The couple are regulars, coming in at least twice a week. You

turn to tomorrow's reservations and see their name there. How do you handle this?

4. You are a CSR in a big company and happen to be walking out the door. A woman close by you slips on some water in the lobby. She is shaken even though she doesn't fall. She starts to complain in a very loud voice. What do you do?

Notes:

_____

_____

_____

_____

_____

_____

_____

_____

_____

_____

_____

_____

_____

_____

_____

_____

_____

_____

_____

SELF-CHECK: The Gift Formula

Why should you start your response to a complaint by saying "Thank you?" List three ways how that opening statement is likely to impact your interaction with your customer.

1. _____

2. _____

3. _____

Which of these tasks do you think is part of your role as a complaint handler? Put a check in the box next to each task that applies to your work.

- ☐ Listen to customers about what they want
- ☐ Identify loyal customers
- ☐ Uncover marketing information
- ☐ Control negative word of mouth
- ☐ Be part of a customer-retention team
- ☐ Pay attention to quality control

When customers complain, how and to whom do you pass information to inside your organization about what you learned? If this is something that doesn't happen in your company, how can you start doing this?

_____

_____

_____

CHAPTER 6

Building Empathy

Empathy is a skill. It's also the foundation for excellent complaint handling.

Some people are better at empathy than others. Whether you have the natural ability to empathize or only a little, everyone can improve this skill. It's like in-line skating: If you skate every day, you will get better. You may never be a champion, but you can unquestionably improve.

In the same way, by practicing the components of empathy, you can learn how to emotionally tune in with your customers.

42

The Power of Empathy

Your empathy tells customers that you understand what they feel. Regardless of the service or product you support, you have a tremendous opportunity to enhance your relationship with your customers by using the skill of empathy.

You can also create stronger bonds by learning to listen with empathy to everyone—complaining customers, internal colleagues, and even customers who want to praise you.

LTIO: How do you define empathy? Be as specific as you can. List any components of empathy you can think of. For example, empathy is the ability to understand someone else's feelings.

1. _____

2. _____

3. _____

What will happen to how you relate with your customers if you connect to them with empathy?

_____

_____

Psychologist Carl Rogers wrote about the power of empathy, "A high degree of empathy in a relationship is possibly the most potent . . . factor in bringing about change and learning."[1]

Do you want your customers to change as they deliver a complaint, maybe from being uncooperative to cooperative? Empathy can make that happen.

Notes:

_____

_____

_____

_____

_____

_____

_____

_____

_____

_____

_____

_____

_____

_____

_____

_____

_____

ACTIVITY

43

Empathy Is as Important as Refunds

Many people think the solution to a service failure is to throw money at the problem. "Give them a refund" or "Give them a discount on a future purchase" seems to be a standard answer. However, being empathic while listening to the customer often has a bigger emotional impact than compensating to solve a problem.

Discounts are always nice, and refunds without hassle are even nicer. However, it may not be enough if that is all that is offered. Customers may think that you are just trying to buy their good feelings, and they may walk away even more disappointed than if you had given them nothing.

Showing up for the customer with a spirit of generosity and empathic listening allows you to build on the partnership between the two of you and increase loyalty.

LTIO: What two things can you do to empathize with your customers when they have experienced a problem? We've provided two example situations.

Situation 1—A customer shows up for an appointment and is kept waiting. How can you both show empathy and let them know that next time you'll call to let them know if your office is running late?

1. _____

2. _____

Situation 2—A customer calls about a mistake on their most recent invoice. It messed up their bookkeeping and also caused their credit score to drop. How can you both show empathy and let them know that it won't happen again?

1. _____

2. _____

Notes:

_____

_____

_____

_____

_____

_____

_____

_____

_____

_____

_____

_____

_____

_____

_____

_____

Reading Emotions

Humans primarily display emotions on their faces in split seconds. If you want to show empathy, you need to read emotions quickly.

Our ability to read subtle displays of emotions influences how we relate to each other. But, of course, you need to be able to see faces to do this. Second best is listening as you can hear emotions in people's voice, pauses, and speed.

By shifting our flexible facial skin, even with only forty-four facial muscles, we can express more than five thousand expressions! Some are easy to read, such as a big, happy smile. Anger is the easiest emotion to read by children, but people have been successful in identifying smiles at three hundred feet, or about the length of a football or soccer field.[2]

Paul Ekman, professor at San Francisco State University, has reduced the long list of emotions to just six. His six basic emotions—*anger, disgust, fear, sadness, surprise, and happiness*—are experienced by everyone and are easily and quickly read across all cultures worldwide.[3]

LTIO: Go to www.ciag.online/44. List the dominant emotion you see on the six pictures in the exercise—one for each of Ekman's six basic emotions. Then in the following six activities, you will read a complete description of these six basic emotions. This is an excellent start for learning how to recognize basic emotions quickly.

ACTIVITY

45

Anger

Anger is usually not subtle. It's nearly impossible to ignore if a person is furious. Sometimes anger shows itself in subtle ways, though you will generally see a clenched jaw, narrowed eyes, or brows that come together that make a wrinkle appear in the middle of the forehead. When people are angry, the chin juts forward, and their mouth turns downward. Some people show several of these signals. Sometimes customers don't like to display anger, but it can leak out onto their faces with tiny telltale signs that CSRs can pick up if they watch carefully.

Many people will also bring their eyebrows together when they are puzzled. If you have this habit, a customer reading your face may think you are annoyed with them because they see anger. People who interact with customers in person need to be careful about furrowing their brows.

LTIO: In the square below, draw one or several pictures of someone who is angry. Sketch a face using the clues above. Don't worry about your artistic talents.

Sadness

Most people readily recognize a down-turned mouth as an expression of sadness. The eyes tend to move down as well. There is nothing "up" in an expression of sorrow; it's all "down."

Many people will sigh if they are sad or their breath will be shaky. At times, if you look closely, you can begin to see their chin shake. Sadness is not an emotion that most people want to repeat—especially in public. When people don't want to show their sadness, they will hold their face tight so no quivering occurs. They may become silent because talking could set off tears.

Sadness is not one of the good emotions to see on a customer's face, especially when they are leaving.

LTIO: In the square below, draw a picture of someone who is sad. Draw one face that depicts just sadness. Then draw another with a combination of sadness and anger, which frequently happens. Use the clues above, and revisit your drawings of anger as well.

Fear

Fear is not an emotion many complaint handlers see unless they are delivering extremely bad news. Sometimes this happens if the customer has to return to work and deliver bad news to their boss about what you have offered as a complaint resolution.

Health-care personnel may see it if they have to deliver bad health news to someone, even if it isn't the organization's fault. Sometimes when a telephone call is about the size of a bill, a customer will become anxious. Sometimes bank officials may see glimmers of fear when they deliver bad financial news based on a customer's credit rating.

Under most circumstances, you won't see the fear that is so extreme that someone's hair stands on end, but you may be able to sense the hairs raising on their body.

You will be able to see eyes that open up wide, with the brows raised and brought together. Most people will open their mouths, perhaps in anticipation of screaming or running away. Fortunately, fear is an emotion not too many CSRs see daily.

LTIO: In the square below, draw one or more pictures, of someone showing fear.

Disgust

When looking for signs of disgust, pay attention to your customer's nose. The nose always wrinkles or the nostrils flare when people experience disgust. Sometimes it can be just a tiny flaring of the nostrils for a brief moment. That tiny movement can tell you that the person you are talking with is disgusted.

Extreme disgust may be indicated by sticking the tongue out. Some people will even make a "yuck" sound so there's no doubt about their feelings.

The eyes also narrow when disgust is experienced. The cheeks lift, and the upper lip is pushed upward.

Disgust may register if you disappoint a customer. They not only feel disappointed but disgusted that this has happened—again. Disgust is often followed by anger. You'll know you're in trouble when customers show you a disgusted signal.

LTIO: In the square below, draw one or more pictures of someone disgusted. Draw a face with slight disgust and then one with a lot of disgust. Again, don't worry about your artistic talents. Sketch pictures using the clues above.

Surprise

Surprise is a close cousin of fear. When people are surprised, the mouth takes on more of a smile shape. The eyes are not as wide open as when someone is afraid, and the jaw drops down even lower than when surprised.

Surprise can change into happiness if the surprise is a positive one. For example, a customer may be surprised if someone tells them the product they just picked up has a flaw. But the surprising news is that the CSR is going to find the customer a perfect replacement that is of higher quality than the original one the customer bought.

Surprise can also happen if the service provider tells the customer that there will be a more extensive selection of colors in the sweaters if they wait until next week or that a sale is about to start, then offering the item the customer wants at 25 percent less. These are good surprise feelings for the beginning of long-term customer loyalty.

LTIO: In the square below, draw a picture of someone who is surprised. Make it a big surprise. Fear is described in Activity 47. Following both sets of clues, you can make sure they look different.

50

Happiness

Happiness is a great emotion to see. It also tends to be contagious, so you may feel it on your face as well. The cheek muscles get involved, pulling the upper corners of the mouth upward. The eyes narrow because the muscles around the corners of the eyes crinkle. Many say you can best detect genuine happiness by watching people's eyes. You can also hear happiness in a person's voice.

It's possible to smile with the mouth and not involve the upper face. You see a false, polite smile if the eyes do not get involved. Crinkle lines will form by the eyes if the happiness expressed is genuine. Try it on your face right now. Put a polite smile on your face and then a genuine one. Notice all the differences that show up on your face with the two different types of smiles.

A genuine smile is the emotion you want your customers expressing when they walk away.

LTIO: In the square below, draw pictures of someone with a polite smile and someone with a genuine smile. Let joy and happiness shine through.

A Case Study in Sharing Emotions

Learning to share emotions effectively is a competency. It can be taught, learned, and then incorporated into your daily behavior. Here is an example of empathy at work.

Financial trust professionals are in the unusual position of creating relationships with customers who typically remain customers until death. Trusts and estate professionals help people arrange their finances to settle everything when they die. Then the professional has to communicate and interact with the relatives of the deceased to make sure everything is carried out as planned by their loved ones. Few professions demand such a high degree of empathy, and one would think that trust professionals would be prepared for the levels of emotionality their customers display.

Nonetheless, one survey revealed that 84 percent of financial trust clients felt their trust professional did not understand the pain they went through after their loved one died. In other words, they didn't think the professional showed any empathy.

This lack of understanding prompted most of these customers to want to work with someone else for their future financial needs. They specifically said they wanted to switch.

The trust officers themselves also felt overwhelmed. They formed close relationships with their clients, and many were distressed when they died. But they all behaved as if nothing unusual had happened. The trust officers thought this was how they "should" behave—that is, not to show any compassion.

One financial institution offered their trust professionals grief training to learn how to react to the beneficiary's pain. They would also learn how to more honestly deal with the pain they themselves felt.

After the training, the customers no longer felt their pain was ignored, and they didn't want to switch to another company.

Another trust and estate company worked with Janelle to learn how to write more sympathetic complaint response letters when beneficiaries complained something hadn't been handled. Janelle taught them how to use the Gift Formula and encouraged them to show empathy and compassion.

Again, after being showed more compassion, the company's customers no longer felt like they wanted to look elsewhere to get their trust and estate needs met.

LTIO: Do you think showing empathy is your responsibility? While you may not deal with life and death issues, every complaint handler has to deal with problems and the emotions of customers who are experiencing loss. Write how you could respond with compassion in the following four situations:

A customer is emotional because they didn't get to their destination on time as their flight was delayed or canceled. What could you say to show compassion?

_____

_____

A customer is irritated because a particular product is not available. What could you say to show empathy?

_____

_____

A customer is upset with a computer problem that feels insurmountable. What could you say to show concern?

_____

_____

A customer feels rejected when they are turned down for a bank loan. They feel the reason for the loan rejection was unfair. What could you say to convey compassion?

_____

_____

Notes:

_____

_____

_____

_____

_____

_____

_____

_____

_____

_____

_____

_____

_____

_____

What's My Impact on My Customers?

Many of us define what we do at work as the functions we perform. For example, many complaint handlers define their work in the following ways:

- "I identify and fix computer problems."
- "When customers complain about incorrect billings, I check invoices."
- "I take back products that customers don't want and refund their money."

All this could be true, but it doesn't describe the impact of these tasks on customers.

Imagine if a customer could rewrite the CSR's job description in terms of impact on them, the customer, what would they say? Here's an example. You troubleshoot credit card issues, such as fraudulent use of credit cards. Your impact description might be "I enable my customers to breathe a sigh of relief knowing that we have their back when a thief uses their credit card to charge things they didn't buy."

This is the emotional component of complaint handling for customers.

LTIO: In one sentence, write a description of how your work affects your customers from your customers' point of view. Do this about two different aspects of your customer work.

1. Describe one task you perform as a service representative or complaint handler.

_____

_____

Now write the impact this part of your work has on your customers. You can start your one-sentence description with the following words: "I help my customers," or "I enable my customers."

_____

_____

2. Now describe another piece of your work you do for customers.

_____

_____

Write the impact of your work on these customers.

_____

_____

LEARNING POINT: We do things for our customers, but sometimes we forget the impact our help has on them. And it's this impact that has a profound emotional effect on our customers.

Notes:

_____

_____

_____

_____

What's Important to My Customers?

If you know what is essential to your customers in various circumstances, you can better empathize with them. Read the following examples and put yourself in the customers' shoes. If you like, you can substitute examples if ours don't match what you do.

LTIO: List at least two concerns your customers might have. You can share your answers with someone else to see if they agree.

Parents with three children are eating at a fast-food restaurant. One child spills a drink. What's important to these customers?

1. _____

2. _____

You have run out of a particular product that is incredibly popular at this time of the year. What's important to the customer who wants this product?

1. _____

2. _____

A shipping company has lost an essential package for a customer. What's important to this customer in this situation?

1. _____

2. _____

LEARNING POINT: If you regularly practice asking yourself, "What's important to my customers?" you're beginning to listen with empathy. It's almost as if you are reading their minds.

Notes:

_____

_____

_____

_____

_____

_____

_____

_____

_____

_____

_____

_____

_____

_____

_____

_____

SELF-CHECK: Building Empathy

When you see a customer having an angry reaction, how should you respond? Rank the following responses from best to worst. Discuss your choices with a partner.

- ☐ Identify what the customer is likely feeling.
- ☐ Tell them what they are feeling is normal.
- ☐ Explain that yesterday another customer had a much worse time with their problem.
- ☐ Tell the customer they should get control of themselves or you won't be able to help them.
- ☐ Simply observe until you can see what the customer will do next.
- ☐ Apologize that you made them angry.
- ☐ Ask for help from your supervisor.
- ☐ Use the Gift Formula, and start by saying "Thank you."

Without referring to the pages in this chapter, verbally describe what each of the six basic emotions look like. Explain how you might confuse them with each other.

- Anger
- Sadness
- Fear
- Disgust
- Surprise
- Happiness

CHAPTER 7

Questioning Skills

There's no better way to learn from the person you are helping than by asking questions.

However, questions are loaded with potential dangers. They can be seen as: invasive, nosey, inappropriate, touching on sensitive issues.

For this reason, questions are best used as reflections of your curiosity. Ask questions to let your customers know you are interested in them.

54

The Power and Challenge of Asking Questions

Long monologues by customers could mean several things, such as this is just how they talk or they want to talk with the CSR. Whatever the cause, in-person or on the telephone, speech that goes on and on is unpleasant at best.

However, by asking your customers questions, you can

- Open your discussion and keep your communication fresh
- Spark customer interest because questions activate the brain
- Keep the complaint-handling session directed toward a goal
- Influence the course and content of the service recovery session
- Encourage reflection and a willingness for them to let you join in communicating and receiving new ideas and information
- Expand possible limited horizons by asking stretch questions
- Gain a feeling of mutual respect and esteem because you cared enough to ask
- Create constructive dialogue from repetitive customer monologues

At a minimum, asking questions will make your service-recovery calls more alive and interesting. Of course, it is not sufficient to just have a list of questions to ask. On one hand, communication is important, but on the other hand, you must adapt your language, choice of words, and behavior to the person you are questioning. Finally, asking the correct type of question for the situation is vital. Doing all this is not easy. It requires alertness, the ability to think clearly and quickly, and sensitivity toward the person you are questioning.

LTIO: Imagine you have been talking with a customer who is telling you how uncomfortable their hotel room was—for the third time. What can you say and what questions can you ask to move this conversation along?

_____

_____

_____

_____

Notes:

_____

_____

_____

_____

_____

_____

_____

_____

_____

_____

_____

_____

Types of Questions

Let's look at a few of the many types of questions. Most CSRs find a couple of questions that work well for them, and they stick with them. In doing so, they miss the benefits and effects of other types of questions. The key to getting better at asking questions is to note the effects they have when you use them.

LTIO: Questions can be easily divided into five types. Basic questions that start with *who*, *what*, *when*, *how*, and *why* are usually either closed or open questions. Let's explore the effects of various questions.

Closed questions—Closed questions can generally be answered with a yes or no. "Did you look at the printed instructions included in the package?"

What are at least two effects of asking closed questions? List one positive effect and one negative effect.

Positive effect: _____

Negative effect: _____

Open questions—Open questions typically require more than a simple yes or no response: "What happened after you did this?" and "What do you think about how the device works?" What's positive and negative about using open-ended questions?

Positive effect: _____

Negative effect: _____

Reflective/leading questions—Reflective questions require the person to think. They can also lead a person to your desired answer: "Did you say that . . . ?" and "If I understand you correctly, you believe that . . . ?" What's positive and negative about leading questions?

Positive effect: _____

Negative effect: _____

Alternative questions—Alternative questions provide at least two choices. Because of this, they can also be leading: "Do you believe this . . . or perhaps you think that . . . ?" What's positive and negative about alternative questions?

Positive effect: _____

Negative effect: _____

Suggestive/trick questions—Suggestive or trick questions either put words into someone's mouth or twist the content: "So you are saying that . . . ?" and "So you really believe that . . . ?" What's positive and negative about suggestive/trick questions?

Positive effect: _____

Negative effect: _____

LTIO: Make a list of these types of questions. The next time you are with a customer, ask at least one of each of these, but not the trick questions. Check your written list whenever you ask one of these questions. Describe the effect of each on your customers. It's clear that each type of question will help get you different results. On the lines below, jot down what happened with each type of question you asked of your customers.

Closed question: _____

_____

Open question: _____

_____

Reflective/leading question: _____

_____

Alternative question: _____

_____

Notes:

_____

_____

_____

_____

_____

_____

_____

_____

_____

_____

_____

_____

_____

Types of Helpful Probing Questions

Questions are helpful if they do the following:

- Help your customer out of a cycle of misunderstanding
- Help your customer out of a limited view of the problem
- Fill the gap when understanding is lacking

Questions can be unhelpful if you're asking them for any of these reasons:

- You feel uncomfortable with silence and fill space with questions
- You are impatient with the speed of the statement of the problem
- You want to put your competence or knowledge on display
- You want to hide your disapproval

Unhelpful questions typically make the customer feel stupid or pushed. Helpful questions about service or product failure belong to the following four types.

1. *Helicopter questions*—"Let's look at this from another perspective." If the customer gets lost in detail, you can suggest looking at their issue from a higher viewpoint. You can ask one of the following questions:

    - "What is the hardest problem you are seeing with the application?"

- "What change could help you feel more in control?"
- "If we solved this problem, would you be completely satisfied?"
- "What is your main reason for considering this change?"
- "What other factors need to be taken into account?"
- "Is there anyone else connected to this issue who has something to say?"

2. *Treasure-hunting questions*—"Let's go back for a moment." After listening to a lengthy description of a problem, you may have the impression that a particular detail was considered too quickly by your customer, and this detail could be crucial. After waiting for an appropriate moment, stop the customer and ask their opinion about the importance of this detail. Here are some examples of treasure-hunting questions:

- "How is this different from what usually happens?"
- "You used the same phrase twice. Are these situations related in your opinion?"
- "I want to understand exactly what you are thinking. I sense you think this is unfair. Can you tell me why?"

3. *Blank spot questions*—"I'm not sure we covered that. Can we look again?" If you don't understand the logic or link between the details you heard while giving full attention to your customer, you may have discovered a contradiction. It could also be an uncovered fact or something that confuses you. It's a blank spot for you. You don't need to hide your lack of understanding as it may lead you to the heart of the problem. Here are some examples of blank-spot questions:

- "Could you tell me how today's situation relates to what happened last year?"

- "I wonder why you hesitated to finish this sentence. What were you thinking?"
- "I am surprised that you called yourself helpless in this case. What stands in the way of us making this work for you?"

4. *Why questions*—"Why did you think that?" Communication experts suggest not asking why questions if there is a chance such a question could be heard as blaming. A blaming question could be "Why didn't you read the instructions?"

How a question is interpreted is mostly determined by the tone of your voice. If the question "Why?" might be seen as blaming, it should be replaced with "What's the reason for . . . ?" A nonjudging why question is not offensive if you are looking for reasons you don't understand. When this occurs, you can also say, "Tell me about this." While it's not a question, it serves the same purpose.

LTIO: You will need a partner to complete this activity. Your partner will play the role of the customer. Define an issue the customer is bringing to you. Choose a complaint you've heard before so you can concentrate on your questions.

Ask four probing questions that fall into each of these four categories. After each question, ask for feedback from your partner. How did your partner feel hearing your question? Did they sense that you had their interests at heart when you asked your questions? How did you feel asking these probing questions? Write down your observations.

1. Helicopter: _____

2. Treasure hunting: _____

3. Blank spot: _____

4. Why: _____

Best Questions for Getting More Customer Feedback

If you ask for your customer's feedback, you are—in most cases—asking for complaints. As we've said, that's a good thing because we can't correct issues if we don't know what they are.

Almost all of us know that a powerful question can completely shift a conversation. It can uncover unspoken messages and help clarify and gather additional customer feedback. You can also get a strong sense of how your customer feels about what has happened.

However, most people are not comfortable with asking questions. This may be partly because the other half of asking questions is listening. Also, questions that attempt to gather additional customer information—or feedback—typically are probing questions. Perhaps you feel you shouldn't be prying into your customer's life. Our experience is that as a complaint handler, the expectation is that you will be asking probing questions. As long as you aren't offensive, go ahead and ask. Be curious.

Go through these questions, highlight a few, and start using them until you become comfortable asking them. You'll notice that most of these questions have an emotional component to them. They are not, by and large, technical product questions. Gradually, add more questions that you can use.

Questions identifying your customer's issue can include these:
- "What do you make of this situation?"
- "How do you feel about . . . ?"

- "What concerns you the most about . . . ?"
- "What seems to be the biggest problem?"
- "What is your main or biggest issue?"
- "What do you think about doing it this way?"
- "How can I help? What seems to be the trouble?"

Questions and prompts about customer satisfaction:
- "Have there been any additional problems with this device?"
- "Can you tell me what you mean by . . . ?"
- "Tell me more about . . ."
- "What other ways have you tried so far?"
- "Can you tell me about the help you received last time you called?"
- "Tell me more about . . ."
- "Anything else? What else?"

Questions that encourage examination of action outcomes:
- "What do you want to happen?"
- "What is your desired outcome?"
- "What do you propose? What is your plan?"
- "If you do this, how will it affect . . . ?"
- "What else do you need for me to consider?"
- "How do you want this action to turn out?"
- "What benefits would you like to get out of what we do?"

Questions that will support learning about your customer:
- "What aspects of this situation bother you?"
- "What do you see as the critical parts here?"
- "How does this fit in with your current priorities?"
- "What excites you about this?"
- "What would be the cost to your team of not taking this action?"

Questions that encourage looking beyond problems and considering future possibilities:

- "What might this situation look like in a few weeks, months, or years from now?"
- "What would be the ideal way to plan for our next steps?"
- "What would be a satisfying way to get there?"
- "If you did it this way, what would the result be?"
- "What do you want—not today but, say, in a year from now?"

LTIO: Choose two questions from above, and use them in an upcoming session with a customer or in a practice session with a partner.

In addition to asking the two questions you choose, make sure you learn how your customer feels when they leave you or you conclude your telephone conversation. You may not like all the answers you receive when you ask these questions.

It would be good to follow up with customers who were left feeling unsatisfied if this happens. Their attitude could change once they have had some time to think about your help. It's important that you do not show fear when your customer responds. If they tell you their truth, they feel open and comfortable with you. That's good for relationship building—as long as you don't get defensive about their answer.

Track your questions and customer responses until you feel comfortable your questions have been fully answered.

List the two questions you will start to focus on to get more customer feedback.

1. _____

2. _____

Describe your customer's reactions to your use of these questions.

1. _____

2. _____

SELF-CHECK: Questioning Skills

What do you gain by asking questions of your customers? List five advantages to asking questions.

1. _____
2. _____
3. _____
4. _____
5. _____

What are the advantages of asking closed yes or no questions?

1. _____
2. _____

What are the advantages of asking open questions?

1. _____
2. _____

Why should you avoid asking trick questions?

1. _____
2. _____

CHAPTER 8

Listening Skills

Listening is a skill. Generally, it's not taught in school. Teachers or professors test around the edges of listening. On exams, students are asked questions to see if they heard what the teacher said.

Many people assume listening is a fixed skill—that is, we were born with the knowledge of how to hear, and you're either good at it or not.

Interestingly, listening is simple. Practice is essential. Honing this skill takes hard work, but it's not complex.

What Does Listening Mean to Me?

Do you want to be a better listener? Listening requires your attention. It means listening to content, how the content is told, and how the person speaking uses their body to communicate.

LTIO: What does listening mean to your work? What percentage of your time do you spend listening to someone else?

_____

_____

Research studies that give people something to listen to and then test them reveal that humans remember only about 50 percent of what they heard. After eight hours, they will remember about one-third of what they heard. Yet these people believe they are good listeners.

Active listening means you listen without judging and without figuring out what you will say next or when you can jump into the conversation. Active listening also means inferring what the speaker means beyond their spoken words.

LTIO: What do you think is required to listen well? Patience is one example. List two others:

1. _____

2. _____

ACTIVITY

59

Listening at Three Levels

The CoActive Training Institute, a top American professional coaching certification organization, teaches three listening levels.[1] You can think of these levels as filters through which listening occurs. We'll cover the first two levels as it takes a bit of practice to get to the third level.

Level I: Listening To—At the first level of listening, you primarily listen to content. This level is where note-taking is crucial, specifically about what the other person says. You should have little difficulty remembering someone's words if you take notes. Take as many notes as you can; more notes are better.

If you want to take notes on your computer, you can do so as long as your computer doesn't make clicking sounds so as to not annoy customers. Zoom has upgraded its platform with a background-noise cancellation feature, which is switched on by default. Many studies show that taking notes on paper helps you remember better, but will you take down more words when entering them on a computer?[2] The choice is yours. Remember to tell your customer you are taking notes; otherwise, they might think you aren't paying attention. You also need to listen to your own internal conversation at this level. What are you saying to yourself?

Level II: Listening For—At the second level, you are listening for what the person possibly means underneath their words. When you take notes on paper, draw a line down the middle of the sheet and put your "listening for" notes side by side with the main content. Many of these listening-for notes might be in the form of questions, such as "What did they mean?"

LTIO: The next time you listen to a customer, set yourself up for note-taking, whether on a computer or paper. Tell your customer you'll be taking notes, then begin. Observe the improvements in your ability to stay focused, remember what was said, and ask better questions.

Notes:

_____

_____

_____

_____

_____

_____

_____

_____

_____

_____

_____

_____

_____

_____

_____

_____

_____

60

Paraphrasing Helps!

Paraphrasing is a restatement of a conversation in different words.

LTIO: You'll need a partner for this activity.

1. Ask your partner to talk for about two minutes on a subject on which the two of you disagree. Don't take any notes: just listen.
2. Then paraphrase what you heard—without giving any additions, showing your emotions, or revealing your position. Just listen and paraphrase; don't repeat word for word but instead what you heard using different words.
3. If your partner feels they were accurately paraphrased—without any side comments or emotions, just facts—then you have finished the first practice session. Try it again so you have at least two practice sessions on different topics.
4. If your partner feels that you didn't accurately cover everything they said, or you put a different spin on their words, then do it again until your partner agrees that all you did was paraphrase.
5. If you are both going through this workbook, you should take turns paraphrasing.

When you practice listening with attention, you have to stay completely focused. You will probably find this hard—everyone does!

LTIO: What's the challenge with paraphrasing?

_____

_____

Why is this skill set critical in complaint handling?

_____

_____

How much do you allow your interpretations to get in the way of clearly understanding what someone else is saying?

_____

_____

Notes:

_____

_____

_____

_____

_____

_____

_____

_____

_____

_____

61

Listening to Deepen Rapport

In activities 30, 31, and 32 we discussed how rapport exists when two people develop a shared feeling of positive communication.

When you listen to someone, you choose between two ways of communicating: you can (1) decide to concentrate on the differences between you, or (2) emphasize the similarities between you. In the latter method, you focus on the topics you agree on, your past experiences, and the things you share in common, especially your shared goals.

You may be thinking, "Wait a minute! What goals do I share with my customers?" You share at least one goal—you both want this complaint handled

- As respectfully as possible, even if your customer wants to vent. Respect can more easily follow if you start by saying hello to your customer in a positive, upbeat way.
- Quickly, with speed. If your customer says, "I'm in a real rush today," you can create rapport, by saying, "Great! Let's get right to it."
- So no additional problems are created. In other words, you both want the complaint to be solved accurately. You can create rapport with your customer by checking, "Does this suggestion sound right to you?"
- In a way that leaves both of you feeling good. Set this as your goal, and you'll probably find that the feeling of positive communication will happen naturally.

LTIO: By this time in the workbook, you probably have upward of a dozen or more things to try out. We recommend writing these ideas on a sheet of paper and putting it somewhere you can see it. The next time you begin to interact with your customer, choose one of these ideas and focus on making sure that goal gets achieved in your conversation.

Notes:

_____

_____

_____

_____

_____

_____

_____

_____

_____

_____

_____

_____

_____

_____

_____

_____

62

Listening by Using Pacing

Pacing is probably one of the best tools to deepen rapport. To use the concept of pacing is to hold up a mirror to another person so they see in your actions and statements a duplicate of their own.

Pacing is not mimicking or aping. It's subtle because the moment the other person sees you mimicking them, the game is over, they will know what you are doing.

Pacing is, therefore, a question of gently entering into another person's expression of the world by mirroring their body language, voice, vocabulary, and mood. Here are two points to understand about pacing.

- Pacing occurs *unconsciously* when people like each other or have been friends for a while. The two people understand each other. When people are in love, any outsider can see evidence of pacing in their body language.
- Pacing can be used *consciously* when rapport does not exist naturally. Pacing creates a feeling of "I know you, and I like you." Nothing has to be said about the fact that you may have just met each other. Two strangers can achieve this same feeling of knowing each other because they are pacing each other.

The highest goal in communication is to achieve rapport. One of the best tools for this is pacing.

What can you pace? Obviously, it makes a difference whether you are virtual or in person. But even while communicating through a chat box, you can mirror speech patterns and feelings. You can also practice pacing the three observable behaviors listed below wherever you are; it doesn't have to be with a customer.

- *Body language*—You can pace a sitting or standing position, movement, position of the legs, arm movements, overall posture, head angle, and facial expression.
- *Speech*—You can pace speed, tone, volume, and choice of words.
- *Words*—You can pace attitudes, beliefs, enthusiasm, tolerance, and feelings.

LTIO: The next time you are with a customer, pace their body language, speech, or words. What happened? How did pacing help you listen? What was the mood you created?

_____

_____

_____

_____

Notes:

_____

_____

_____

_____

_____

_____

_____

SELF-CHECK: Listening Skills

What are three differences between "listening to" and listening for"?

1. _____

2. _____

3. _____

Which is more important as a complaint handler, "listening to" or "listening for"? Why? Yes, they are both important, but choose one and make an argument for that type of listening.

_____

_____

_____

_____

What are three reasons why being able to paraphrase what a customer says is important? What advantages will you have if you can paraphrase accurately?

1. _____

2. _____

3. _____

CHAPTER 9

Beyond Words

If you understand the underlying mechanisms contributing to complaint-handling success, you will begin to see complaint handling as a puzzle. Just as every puzzle is different, every complaint is different. Some are easy, and others are complicated and not readily put together.

Remember, a message is being exchanged between you and your customer. Reading body language is a good skill to develop because sometimes the body says one thing and the words say another. When this happens, you need to pay close attention to body language.

Generally, body language speaks that person's truth. As a result, we need to pay careful attention using our eyes. This chapter will look at different aspects of body language.

63

What's the Body Saying?

One of the most important details to look for when receiving feedback or a complaint is body language. As people say all the time, actions speak louder than words.

When we talk about body language, we are talking about body movement and how people say what they say.

LTIO: We've included three options. Try at least one.

1. Go people watching. Sit in a crowded plaza or go out to lunch or dinner and concentrate on other people's body language. Be careful not to stare! Can you guess what they are talking about? Do you have a sense of what they are feeling?
2. Watch a movie or a television commercial you have not seen before without sound, closed captions, or subtitles. Can you figure out what is going on by focusing on what people say with their bodies?
3. Watch a silent movie, especially one starring Charlie Chaplin. We recommend either *Modern Times* or *The Kid*. You could also watch a movie with Laurel and Hardy or the Marx Brothers in it. They can be found on many streaming services and on YouTube. All of them are excellent videos that show the power of body language and can be found at www.ciag.online/63.

What three conclusions can you draw from the three exercises on the previous page? Have a discussion with a partner if you can so someone watches along with you.

1. _____

2. _____

3. _____

It's impossible not to communicate. We constantly communicate, even when we are not talking, as you saw in the exercises above.

The question to keep foremost in your mind is, What is my customer telling me beyond the words they are speaking? It is essential to look at body language to get a complete message. It helps solve the puzzle for understanding your customers.

LTIO: Think about and answer the following questions: How much attention do you pay to body language? How much significance do you give to this important part of communication? Do you ever find yourself saying, "But you said . . ." and the other person responds, "Yes, but what I meant was . . ."?

_____

_____

_____

_____

_____

Body Language Rules and Cues

Three rules will help you to interpret body language:

1. Look at the whole message, not just one part of the body.
2. Relate the message to the context. Is someone crossing their arms because it is cold or because they are withdrawing from you?
3. Look at a combination of three body movements in the same direction. For example, a person is clearly annoyed with how much time you are taking if their arms are crossed, they look annoyed, and they keep glancing at their watch.

Joe Navarro, an expert in body language and author of several books and videos about the topic, talks about comfort and discomfort and how these emotions show up in our body language. He explains why we bite our lips: it's to calm down and is a substitute for sucking our thumb as we did when we were children.

Navarro also says we cover our ears when we hear something we don't like. When we put our lips together, we're saying something is wrong. We also move our lips to the side when we disagree. Navarro also talks about deception and how to spot it in "The Power of Nonverbal Communications—CMX Summit West 2015": www.ciag.online/64.

LTIO: *Wired* produced an excellent series of videos with Navarro, which you can find here: www.ciag.online/64-b. Watch these videos and write down what the body language of the complainer is telling you.

Video 1's body language: _____

_____

Video 2's body language: _____

_____

Video 3's body language: _____

_____

Notes:

_____

_____

_____

_____

_____

_____

_____

_____

_____

_____

_____

_____

_____

Our Voice and Its Hidden Subtleties

The way we say what we say is important. Have you noticed that you can tell if a person is smiling or angry even while talking on the phone? As complaint handlers, we need to hear the subtext—to listen beyond the words. Your customer might say, "Yes, that solution is okay," but they don't mean it, and you can hear the difference.

Jim Clemente, a former FBI agent, explains how to detect lying and deception. You can see signs of deception not only by reading body language but also by listening to how people say what they say: www.ciag.online/65.

LTIO: Go to www.ciag.online/65-b and listen to the four different voice messages as if you were listening on the phone. Each message uses the same phrase. Your task is to indicate whether the speaker's meaning is the same in all four messages. Write down your thoughts on the chart below while you listen to each of them.

Audio	What words are being said?	What emotions do you hear?
1		
2		
3		
4		

Check to see if your notes coincide with ours at www.ciag.online/65-c.

LEARNING POINT: Sometimes it's easy to perceive what the other person means beyond the words they use, especially when it is as obvious as in the audios shared above. In real life, however, it might be a little more difficult, but it's a skill you can develop with practice. Start to pay attention to body language and voice intonation. Once that becomes a habit, you will find you are better able to detect the meaning behind the words.

Notes:

_____

_____

_____

_____

_____

_____

_____

_____

_____

_____

_____

_____

_____

_____

_____

SELF-CHECK: Beyond Words

When looking at body language or listening to someone talking, what three rules should you observe?

1. _____

2. _____

3. _____

When someone's body language does not support the words they are saying, what should you give greater weight to? Why?

_____

_____

Remember the six basic emotions we covered in chapter 6: Happiness, surprise, disgust, anger, fear, and sadness? What do each of these sound like based on your own experience?

- Happiness sounds like _____
- Surprise sounds like _____
- Disgust sounds like _____
- Anger sounds like _____
- Fear sounds like _____
- Sadness sounds like _____

CHAPTER 10

Powerful Phrases That Work

How many times have you heard someone say, "I'll never forget what my grandmother/father/brother/boss/colleague said to me. It's had an impact on me that has lasted forever."

But how often do we say, "I'll never forget what a customer-service representative said when I complained. It completely turned me around. I'll never forget it."

We don't hear that too often! Why not? We have a chance to say something to our customers that matters. It's our chance to have a lasting effect.

ACTIVITY

66

Words Matter

Most people don't think that words matter regarding complaint handling. In fact, most people think of complaint handling as transactional. Yes, you can turn a customer-business relationship into something entirely transactional, but that's no fun for the service provider or the customer.

When we give total weight to what words mean, we let customers know we seek a business relationship when we communicate with them. Through this communication we answer questions, fix problems, and form relationships.

LTIO: What words or phrases have you said to a customer in a complaint situation that you know impacted them positively? Write three phrases you know make a positive difference.

1. _____
2. _____
3. _____

What words or phrases have you said to a customer that you know or suspect had a negative impact on the customer? This may require some deeper thinking because we tend to justify our words or don't believe they have as much impact as we realize. List three phrases that might have made your complaint handling more difficult.

1. _____
2. _____
3. _____

67

Powerful Complaint-Handling Phrases

Over many years, CSRs have developed powerful phrases that say to customers, "We want to help you." In this activity, we share phrases that display helpfulness. Highlight the ones that appeal to you.

1. *"Let me see what I can do."*—This phrase is an Apple service term. Janelle has heard it dozens of times when receiving help in Apple Stores or with AppleCare. This phrase means the customer may not get what they want, but it's not an outright rejection. It holds out the hope that something is going to happen.

2. *"Let's work together to make you as satisfied as possible."*—Again, this is not an outright promise to make something happen, but it gets close. The phrase offers an element of hope. These words also speak of partnership: "We're going to do something together."

3. *"Tell me everything that happened."*—When you ask the customer to give you a complete description of what happened, you're saying you have time to listen. Keep in mind that you may spend an extra five minutes with the customer, but what you get back in loyalty is worth much more than what five minutes costs. It is a phrase that also says, "I trust you."

4. *"I know you are going to like this."*—You are affirming the customer's choice. Everyone wants to know they have made a good choice, especially when they aren't sure. If you aren't sure, then don't say this. Use it when you know it will work for them.

5. *"That shouldn't have happened."*—You are saying several things here. First, you are taking responsibility—not necessarily for your role in what happened but that someone in your business

or elsewhere did something, and you want to acknowledge what they said. Second, you are saying that the quality standard of your company is higher than this. You are also implying that whatever happened will be fixed.

6. *"Remember, you'll also need . . ."*—Be sure to tell customers what else they need to make their product work—such as batteries or a particular food to bring out the taste of whatever product you provided them.

7. *"I'll do this . . ."*—Use definite language instead of saying something such as "I might be able to . . . " Wishy-washy language makes customers nervous. Give them a precise time frame or at least one that falls within a time period. Don't say four o'clock when what you mean is somewhere between four and four-thirty. If an exact time is tough for you to confirm, send a text message to tell them you are delayed. Keep communicating!

8. *"You are important to me. I want to do my best for you."*—You have to believe this phrase yourself, or you shouldn't say it. If you can't sound as if you are genuine with some of these phrases, don't use them. Do you truly want to do your best for them? Then say it. The customer will appreciate your assurance.

9. *"I'm glad you called/came in. I want to resolve this for you as soon as possible."*—This phrase is particularly good to use when you know the customer has already spent some time on this problem. Customers like to hear this certainty. Speed sets a tone and shows you value the customer.

10. *"Thank you for your information. With it I should be able to fix this quickly."*—You're doing a couple of things with this phrase: (1) thanking them for helping you with their information and (2) assuring them that something is going to happen.

11. *"Good morning, my name is Sam. How can I help you?"*—Establish your identity. Unless your company has a specific policy of people not using their names, start to build a relationship by exchanging names. This shows that you aren't hiding. Personalize whenever

you can. And make sure it's your name. Janelle often hears Western names when it's clear the person is calling from India.

12. *"You are fantastic. You were so helpful!"*—Brag about them to them: "You were the most clearly spoken customer I've spoken with today," "You were so patient. I can't thank you enough," and "You were very helpful, looking up that extra information so I could quickly help you." Your customers want to know that you appreciate them for who they are. By the way, you don't have to make anything up. There's always something positive to say about someone.

13. *"Let me check on that so I can be sure to get it right."*—Customers don't mind if you don't know everything. It's best not to say, "I don't know." Tell them you will check to make sure you get it right. It's the last part of those two phrases that the customer hears: "get it right."

14. *"Let me tell you what is happening."*—Customers like to be kept in the loop. If they have to wait on the phone before you can get back to them, pop in periodically and tell them what is happening. They will appreciate it. If the customer has to leave to handle something else, they won't lose the connection with you because you'll have a chance to discuss how much longer they will have to hold.

15. *"I'm going to do something special for you."*—Of course, you only want to say this if you will do something special. It doesn't have to be out-of-this-world special, just something they will appreciate. For example, you can give them a number to call you directly or say you will call them back so they don't have to remain on hold.

16. *"You made a good choice."*—Everyone wants to know they chose well. This is especially true if they are a little nervous about purchasing the product and now it has a problem. Assure them that the product is a good one, and even more importantly, that you're going to stand by them until their product is fixed.

17. *"What can I do to help you?"*—It's "I" not "we." People want to feel you are responsible, and saying "I" does that.

18. *"I look forward to seeing you again!"*—If they are talking with you about a complaint, make sure this phrase doesn't sound like you want them to have another problem. You liked "seeing" or "meeting" them because of who they are, and not because of their problems.

19. *"I want to be fair to you. Let me check to see what kind of leeway I have to make this right for you."*—Fairness is critical to customers. They see it as something the company has the power to deliver. Customers feel at the mercy of whether companies will treat them fairly.

20. *"Thank you for telling me. I am so sorry this happened, and I'm going to do everything I can to help you."*—Don't forget the Gift Formula. It's the best set of phrases to display helpfulness right at the beginning!

LTIO: List two phrases you will start to use.

1. _____

2. _____

Describe your customer's reactions to your use of these phrases.

1. _____

2. _____

Notes:

_____

_____

_____

_____

Three Phrases in One

In this series of three phrases, you can identify yourself, describe the action you are taking, and then spell out the value that will happen.

1. *Identity*—Establish what will happen, either in person or leaving a voice message; for example, "Hi, this is Victoria. I'm calling to let you know we are continuing to work on the issue we talked about yesterday."
2. *Action*—Tell them what you will do: "Here's my next step. I'm going to . . ." or "I need from you . . ." or "Do this . . ."
3. *Value*—Make a value statement, such as "This will fix your problem," "I guarantee you will save a lot of time," or "You'll have the replacement product in just a couple of days."

One particularly good way to use this set of three phrases is when you leave a voice-mail message. Think through your identity, action, and value statements so you can record them perfectly. You can use these three statements in the middle of a long call and also to summarize your call at the end. If it helps, write down these action steps and place them by your computer, so you don't have to think of new ones every time you make a call.

LTIO: Describe a situation where you need to get back to your customer on the telephone. Then describe your identity, action, and value statements.

Situation: _____

1. Identity statement: _____

_____

2. Action statement: _____

_____

3. Value statement: _____

_____

Notes:

_____

_____

_____

_____

_____

_____

_____

_____

_____

_____

_____

_____

_____

SELF-CHECK: Powerful Phrases That Work

What are three advantages of using preset phrases showing helpfulness to your customers that you know will work?

1. _____

2. _____

3. _____

What are your absolute favorite phrases that you know will work with your customers?

_____

_____

_____

What are three things to watch out for when using preset phrases showing helpfulness to your customers? What could go wrong?

1. _____

2. _____

3. _____

CHAPTER 11

Difficult Customer Interactions

Everyone runs into upset and angry customers from time to time. CSRs may face more angry customers than many other essential service staff. Some days CSRs must wonder if a single nice person is left in the world.

The key is to know how to best react and not take animosity personally. We'll show you how to do both better.

69

Difficult Customers

Many new CSRs do not know how to handle upset, aggressive, complaining customers. Many hold these beliefs:

- The only way CSRs can learn is simply through experience, and that can take years to acquire.
- CSRs pick up their approach to dealing with angry people in their childhood homes. Unfortunately, they learned from their brothers and sisters, who didn't know much about dealing with angry siblings except to get angry back or break into tears.
- Many young CSRs in the 2020s accept attacks by customers as an inherent element of working with the public. Take it, or leave your job, they say.
- Because of how they are treated by some customers, it's normal for many CSRs to go home at night, sit in their bathrooms, cry, and remain sleepless throughout the night. They say they feel like quitting after a particularly bruising day.

We hate to agree with the belief that some customers have just become nastier, showing little respect for others. But let's assume this is the reality in today's world. If so, then we really need strong backbones to go home in the evening still feeling emotionally whole.

It's possible to argue that some service providers earn the abuse they receive, which happens from time to time. But in this chapter, we will look at how you can protect yourself from customers' verbal abuse and help them move away from anger.

We distinguish between dissatisfaction and anger. A simple way to look at the differences is that you can have dissatisfaction without anger, but you will not see anger without dissatisfaction in a customer.

LTIO: What three things would you most like to learn about being around angry customers? Let's make sure you get answers for these items.

1. _____
2. _____
3. _____

Notes:

_____

_____

_____

_____

_____

_____

_____

_____

_____

_____

_____

_____

_____

_____

The Emotional Giant—Anger

Volcanos are potent forces of nature. You can't ignore them—especially the giant ones. They are dangerous and gain the entire world's attention.

With volcanos, it's a good idea to move away as there is no way to stop their force. A complaining customer can sometimes be like that.

When faced with an upset and aggressive customer, complaint handlers need to decide whether they are in physical danger, and then they need to act.

Let's take a look at the various levels of anger and upset customers and determine what to do.

Notes:

_____

_____

_____

_____

_____

_____

_____

_____

_____

_____

Anger as a Volcano

Elisabeth Kübler-Ross is known for defining the five stages people go through when grieving: (1) denial, (2) anger, (3) bargaining, (4) depression, and (5) acceptance. These stages help us understand human grief.

The same stages, with a few changes, also apply to anger and rage: (1) denial and shock, (2) blaming, (3) eruption, (4) bargaining, and (5) acceptance.

LTIO: As you look at the images on page 159, do these angry customer reactions look familiar to you? Which do you find most difficult to deal with?

_____

_____

Anger is one of the strongest emotions humans experience. It affects both the angry person and the people who have to endure it. Angry customers tend to be nasty when they complain. After all, how do they show the intensity of their anger without some degree of nastiness?

People get angry to show something is important to them. They think they will be ignored without a display of anger or passed on without being taken care of.

Angry customers may consider acting violently, but mostly they don't. They tend to exaggerate their complaints and make "I'm never coming back" types of threatening comments.

Angry customers think they know who to blame for their situation, and generally, it is the person helping them. The displayed anger frequently gets in the way of the service provider being able to help, so often anger doesn't help most customers get what they want. It's too bad more of them don't know this.

One of the fascinating behaviors of dissatisfied customers who are not angry is that they tend to switch companies in higher percentages than those who are both dissatisfied and angry. This means that a CSR has a better chance of keeping an angry customer. It's more difficult to keep a sullen dissatisfied customer who just threatens to walk away but doesn't display any anger. Therefore, CSRs need to be careful to not contribute to their customer's anger but instead strongly focus on eliminating their dissatisfaction.

Notes:

_____

_____

_____

_____

_____

_____

_____

_____

_____

_____

_____

72

Anger and Dissatisfaction

If you can understand your own behavior in situations where both dissatisfaction and anger appear, you will be able to understand your customers better. Then you can choose the best approach depending on what you see in the customer.

LTIO: Describe an incident where you were dissatisfied, and it ended with you not getting what you wanted. You didn't get angry, but you felt dissatisfied. This example could come from work or your personal life.

What were you thinking while this was happening? First, write what happened, and then second, share your example with someone else to see if they have had a similar type of experience.

_____

_____

_____

_____

Next, describe an incident where you were both dissatisfied and angry, but it ended with you getting what you wanted. This example could come from work or your personal life.

_____

_____

_____

What was different between these two examples?

_____

_____

_____

LEARNING POINT: People get angry to show something is important to them. If the issue is not essential to them, they will probably shrug off the incident or make the decision to walk away.

Let's look at the stages of anger so we can understand how to manage it.

Notes:

_____

_____

_____

_____

_____

_____

_____

_____

_____

_____

_____

_____

_____

73

The First Stage: Denial

You can learn to help someone with their out-of-control anger by visualizing the erupting anger in stages. As mentioned earlier, these stages are similar to the well-known stages of grieving identified by Elizabeth Kübler-Ross, a Swiss psychiatrist. Kübler-Ross shows her stages of grieving as an upside-down U-shaped curve. Interestingly, the same model works for anger with a few adjustments.

We call the first stage the *denial and shock* phase of outrage. You may hear customers say any of the following in this beginning stage of explosive anger: "There's no way this could be true" or "There must be some mistake." People say the same thing when they face sudden grief: "No, it can't be true. Tell me you're kidding." Helping a customer overcome an extreme anger outburst is easier if you catch their anger in the first stage.

Be alert when you hear denial types of statements from customers. They are likely only the opening volley. The customer is still attempting to control their anger, but you are glimpsing the tip of a potential major volcanic eruption. This is what you can do to avoid a big eruption:

1. Answer their questions, look competent, and be at least minimally friendly and helpful. Provide as much information as possible.
2. Support the customer's initial emotional reaction: "Thank you for speaking up. You're right. There must be some sort of mistake. Let's check it out."
3. Involve them in helping you figure out what happened. If you are looking at information on a computer screen, tell your customer

what you are doing or seeing. Don't exclude them. Keep them involved. It helps defuse their anger before it explodes.

LTIO: You'll need to find a partner to try this out. Do this twice so each of you can feel what it is like on both sides of the situation.

Your partner will play the role of a complaint handler. You will play the role of the getting-ready-to-explode customer. Write a question that a customer might ask, demanding that you do something.

_____

_____

The CSR will answer, "No, this is not possible."

This will set you, the customer, into the beginning of your anger. As the customer, you will make denial statements, getting more and more angry as you speak.

The CSR will respond using one or all of the three suggestions above.

As the CSR uses these prompts to respond to you, the customer, check internally to see how you feel as you are being "talked down" by the problem solver. Watch what happens to your anger levels. To get the most out of this LTIO, watch your reactions carefully so you can see how you are affected by the CSR's remarks.

Next, swap roles. This time, you will play the role of the CSR. Your customer partner will ask a question demanding something; you will say, "No, that is not possible." As the CSR, you will attempt to bring the customer back to a position of reduced anger.

When you have both had a chance to play the two roles, discuss what happened. Be aware that if the CSR does not influence the customer, they will become increasingly angry.

The Second Stage: Blaming

In the second stage of anger—the blaming phase—complaint handlers run into the most challenging part of the anger explosion, in which customers will likely go on the attack.

Try to understand what is going on with the customer. They have been denied something important to them, or they have gotten bad news. The next thing they will do is find someone to blame for the situation they are in.

They might say, "I'm not surprised. This happens all the time. Your people are so incompetent." Even though some may not say this out loud, their thought includes you in this group of low-performing idiots. Taking such comments personally can be hard.

All of us who help customers want to be appreciated for our efforts. When we are being blamed, remaining friendly is not easy. In fact, it inspires a need to go on the counterattack. If we appreciate that blaming statements are part of the anger of dissatisfied customers who are at least still communicating with us, perhaps we can avoid getting defensive.

LTIO: Talk through the following first three steps with your partner. You don't have to role-play, just discuss what is happening in this second stage of anger. Try the fourth step as an exercise with a partner.

1. Keep looking at the gift you are being given when you are being blamed and attacked. Ignore the fact that this gift is poorly wrapped. If you dig deep enough, you'll probably find a gift.

2. While a customer is operating from this anger stage, actively listen rather than attempt to say anything. Nod your head as if in agreement or say "hmmm" if you are on the phone with them. Remind yourself, if you can turn an angry customer around, you are more likely to keep them as a long-term customer.

3. When customers are angry, they also tend to become loud. If they think you will brush them off, they tend to get even louder. It's just a nonverbal way to let you know they want you to listen to them. If you are on the phone, you can hold the speaker away from your ears and direct the anger away from you. It's a bit more tolerable that way. If you are in person and other people are around, you can perhaps take the customer to a quiet place so they don't disrupt other people and embarrass themselves.

4. If your customer looks as if they will continue shouting, you can try the following technique. It starts with saying two negative statements and finishing with a positive one. It's like good theater in that it grabs attention, and the listener will begin to wonder what is coming next. Here's what you can say: "I don't care how angry you get with me (the first negative); it's not going to stop me (the second negative) from doing everything I can to help you (the positive)." This statement, like any good exchange, requires a little practice until you can say it fluently and with some meaning. Be sure to put pauses in between each phase so your customer will hear what you are saying.

Notes:

_____

_____

_____

_____

_____

ACTIVITY

75

The Third Stage: Eruption

In the third stage of anger, the eruption phase, customers start to explode. What can the CSR do? Focus on the type and level of how upset they are—though not necessarily their words as they'll try to bait you. This is where techniques come in handy.

One example of a statement designed to pull you into an argument is, "When did you start treating your customers like dogs?" You could respond by saying, "I'm very sorry that we've offended you. We shouldn't have done that." The customer may say, "If you cared even a tiny bit about your customers, you wouldn't have such stupid policies." They are baiting you to say, "But we do care about our customers." This will only give them more ammunition to continue doing battle, and you are then in a defensive position. They'll ask, "Then why . . . ?" And the battle will rage.

LTIO: A better way to respond in this stage is to ask a question about their attack. You could say, "I'm very sorry. What happened that makes you think we don't care about you?" This will surprise them. They expect a defense, not a question. Remember, if you do not defend yourself, the customer will be less likely to continue their assault.

It's also helpful to accept the angry person for who they are and what they are expressing right now. People tend to get stuck when they sense you don't accept them. They want you to hear them. Simply observe their explosion without judgment. We know it's hard, but try it out. Your acceptance can help them change and soften their tone.

The Fourth Stage: Bargaining

In the fourth stage of anger, the bargaining phase, customers start to seek a way to solve their problems. Their rage is subsiding, and they are beginning to use the thinking side of their brains.

They'll say things such as "Well, what are you going to do?" or "Is this the best you can do for me?" This is your opportunity to partner with them and be more active in the conversation. Stay focused on solutions rather than problems. Don't be put off by nasty language. Remember, they are bargaining with you to solve their problem, and they are probably still angry.

An understanding of anger's stages helps explain why sometimes this method does not work. It's tempting to try to move from the first stage to the third or fourth stages to avoid going through the second stage, the blaming phase. But angry people must have at least some expression of all four stages to complete their anger process—just as they do in the grieving process.

People are not rational when they are in the denial and blaming stages. They're more reasonable in the bargaining phase and finally have a chance to integrate what is happening in the acceptance phase, the fifth stage. If you skip one of these stages, the following can happen.

A woman who worked in Janelle's office once had a problem with a shipper. She got the situation worked out—not perfectly, but the package made it to the client, though it was a couple of days late. Janelle's employee, however, was not happy and complained, "She never once apologized. She didn't listen to the 'inconvenience' this caused me. I don't want to use that shipper again." The shipper CSR had tried to go from denial to bargaining, skipping stages two and three. It didn't work.

LTIO: The next time you face an angry customer, let them express their emotions. You can't stop an erupting volcano, but you can observe it and listen. Telling them not to be angry doesn't work. Write down what happens when you give them a chance to express their anger.

_____

_____

_____

Notes:

_____

_____

_____

_____

_____

_____

_____

_____

_____

_____

_____

_____

_____

The Fifth Stage: Acceptance

In the fifth stage of anger, the acceptance phase, you get to find out where the customer is now once the four stages are complete, or at least mostly resolved. Acceptance with complaint handling is different from the kind of acceptance that Kübler-Ross described about grief. Grief associated with the loss of a loved one sometimes never ceases.

As complaint handlers, your goal is to get your customers to move on to accept your solution. They may not get exactly what they wanted, but they can be satisfied with what they get. Their explosion of anger may have been relatively brief, so emotions are still simmering. A complaint handler can help such a customer move on by providing alternatives. Customers may face problems that will never be fully repaired, but alternatives can help. Put your customers in charge of their own solutions as much as possible.

LTIO: Follow-up contact with customers can help. Contact them after a short period of time has passed if the customer was not satisfied with how their complaint was handled while you were talking with them. If you provided an alternative solution because you couldn't give the customer exactly what they wanted, they may realize that what was offered was actually good. Their anger has subsided. You have demonstrated that you care about them. All these combined factors will make it more likely for them to appreciate what you did.

We both have received apologies from customers when they were given a chance to calm down. Most don't want to be your enemy. You can be gracious and say that there is no need to apologize—after all, anyone would have been angry.

Let's Revisit That Volcano

Before we consider other approaches to dealing with anger, let's visit the anger volcano and review what we covered. This model has five steps and several actions that can be taken.

LTIO: Review the model, name the stages, and indicate how to identify the stage of anger the customer is in. Then write what you can do when you encounter someone at that stage. Use the form below to write in your answers.

Don't turn back to the pages and peek so that all you are doing is copying the information in this workbook. Think your way through the volcano, especially about steps you can take to help customers move through the stages. If you think of some action items we didn't present, that's great. Let us know on our web page or Facebook page.

Stage 1: _____

Description of this stage: _____

_____

What you can do: _____

_____

Stage 2: _____

Description of this stage: _____

_____

What you can do: _____

_____

Stage 3: _____

Description of this stage:_____

_____

What you can do: _____

_____

Stage 4: _____

Description of this stage:_____

_____

What you can do: _____

_____

Stage 5: _____

Description of this stage:_____

_____

What you can do: _____

_____

Notes:

_____

_____

_____

_____

_____

_____

No Customer Name-Calling

One of the most damaging practices in organizations is customer name-calling. We're not talking about the names customers are called to their faces. Most service providers are good about not insulting customers to their faces. We automatically recognize that calling another person an unflattering name to their face is socially unacceptable—unless it is done in fun or with affection and with the other person's implicit permission.

We're talking about when CSRs call their customers names behind their backs. One of the reasons why name-calling is so attractive to CSRs is that it's a way to safely get back at customers after a busy, long day or after a difficult interaction. Here are some ways service providers call their customers names:

- They roll their eyes while talking with them on the telephone.
- They write comments about them in their notes on their computers.
- They make rude gestures that only their colleagues can see.
- They swear after they have hung up the phone.
- They call them jerks, idiots, turkeys, animals, creeps, and a few other unprintable names.

Sometimes service providers will call one customer who has just left a name in the presence of another customer. They will say, "What a jerk," as the customer leaves. It's an unusual way to begin a fresh service interaction with another customer!

LTIO: What's your practice? Do you ever call your customers names? List three things you have done. Don't worry about anyone seeing what you write. It's your workbook! We don't think we have ever met a CSR who hasn't done this from time to time.

1. _____

2. _____

3. _____

Notes:

_____

_____

_____

_____

_____

_____

_____

_____

_____

_____

_____

_____

_____

_____

The Case of the Picky Customer

A seminar leader returned to a hotel where he had previously delivered seminars. Upon arrival, he happened to glance at the banquet function sheet the hotel had prepared about his room setup. To his surprise, he saw written in bright bold red letters "PICKY CUSTOMER."

He was embarrassed and didn't say anything about what he saw, but it left him feeling bad about the hotel and not wanting to return. Any of the following ways would be a better way to describe this seminar leader other than "picky":

- "This customer has high and exact standards. Let's meet them!"
- "We can learn from this customer by meeting his high service standards."
- "Service quality is extremely important to this customer."

LTIO: How could each of the customers below be talked about other than to call them names?

Customers are in a hurry. What could they be called rather than angry or pushy customers?

_____

Customers are upset. What could they be called other than rude and inconsiderate?

_____

Patients are sick and hurting. What could they be called other than whiners?

_____

The person you just talked with has a lot of energy. How could they be described other than as "off the wall"?

_____

Customers have to get their package out on time. What could they be called other than impatient jerks?

_____

Your customer needs something to be perfect. How could they be described rather than as a demanding, impossible-to-satisfy person?

_____

Notes:

_____

_____

_____

_____

_____

_____

_____

_____

_____

81

Ensure Your Own Safety

Essential workers and CSRs have unfortunately been physically attacked by customers, so we will share a word about self-protection.

The Crisis and Trauma Resource Institute, located in Winnipeg, Canada, proposes a variety of tips on its website under the heading "Free Resources."[1] If you follow these tips, you will be much more likely to survive an assault on your safety.

LTIO: Keep these tips handy and review them from time to time.

- *Be aware of your environment*—If you find yourself nervous, check your own emotions. How are you feeling? Resist the urge to give in to your fear. Project confidence, scan your environment, and see where the exits are located. If someone seems to be a threat, check to see what they are doing. Are they escalating their behavior? Start to plan how you will escape if necessary.
- *Be careful how you speak*—Speak calmly and slowly. Choose your words wisely. The calmer you stay, the more likely this will lessen the threat. Don't tell anyone to calm down.
- *Acknowledge the situation*—If you get a chance, describe the emotion you see and ask open-ended questions: "You're angry. What's going on?"
- *Shift into a listening stance*—If your arms are crossed at your chest, open them. Raise your eyebrows and make respectful eye contact. Don't stare. Make sounds to indicate you are listening.

- *Be empathetic*—Tell them you will help sort out the situation. Use "we" language.
- *Use silence and pauses to slow things down*—Sometimes violence erupts because things speed up too quickly. You can say, "Give me a second to think about that. You're making an important point."
- *Offer choices*—Many people become violent when they feel backed into a corner. Offer them choices: "Here's what we can do. It's your choice. I'll help you with whatever decision you want to make."

Notes:

_____

_____

_____

_____

_____

_____

_____

_____

_____

_____

_____

_____

_____

_____

SELF-CHECK: Difficult Customer Interactions

If a customer is showing signs of explosive anger, explain why you should let them pass through all five phases of anger. In other words, why shouldn't you push them to quickly accept your solution?

_____

_____

_____

What are three dangers of engaging in customer name-calling?

1. _____

2. _____

3. _____

Customers frequently get irritated with CSRs. But when they move into rage, something different is happening. List five important things to be aware of if a customer looks like they are about to explode.

1. _____

2. _____

3. _____

4. _____

5. _____

CHAPTER 12

Making Stress Work for Me

Stress takes place all the time. In fact, a body without any stress is a dead body, and we don't want that! You always want some stress—not so much that you feel you are carrying the weight of the world on your shoulders, but enough to get the job done.

When you say, "I have a temperature," it doesn't mean you didn't have one before. It means you have a higher than normal temperature.

"I'm feeling stressed" doesn't mean you had no stress before. It means you have more than you want right now.

We'll review how you can handle customer complaints and still not feel stressed.

82

Stress Starts with a Decision

Janelle grew up with stress in her back pocket. It drove her life from an early age, resulting in heart disease, intense competitiveness, and ulcers. She was told that she wouldn't live to thirty if she didn't change her lifestyle. That caught her attention. She began exercising and studied psychology with an emphasis on personal development. She practiced yoga and meditation and slowly began to bring her intense personality under control, and her health improved.

In her early thirties, she suspected there were many other high achievers just like herself. She developed a stress management program, wrote an accompanying book, and offered the program to corporate clients. For years she taught others to be resilient in life. Now she applies the same ideas to be resilient when handling complaints.

Victoria lives in a high-stress city, Mexico City. She moves around from one corporate client to another through massive traffic jams. She manages her thriving business and is highly involved with her family.

We both have had to make some personal decisions about not letting our lives take control over our mental and physical health. We both know that managing stress starts with the decision to have control over your stress reactions. You could say it's a mindset.

Let's start with your definition of stress.

LTIO: Describe what you think stress is. How do you know when you are stressed? Do you think you have any control over your stress?

_____

_____

ACTIVITY

83

What Is Stress?

Simply put, stress is how your body responds to events around it. You can overrespond, underrespond, or respond at the right level. You can also hold on to your response for a longer time period than is necessary. For example, some people have a bad day at work, and at night they do not sleep well. They have a bad customer interaction, and they brood over it for the rest of the day. They get overwhelmed with all the calls coming in and take it out on their family that evening. Is this anything you do?

Stress can happen in the following circumstances:

- You have to act to save your life.
- You compete for a prize (especially if you win).
- You exercise or participate in sports.
- You get married or are promoted in your job.

Your body is built for stress. Your body, however, is not made for high levels of stress over a long period.

Positive stress can help you do the following:

- Master complex tasks more easily.
- Experience a heightened sense of stimulation about your life.
- Think more clearly because your brain makes quicker decisions.
- Have a better chance of saving your life in a dangerous situation.

Unfortunately, stress also happens in the following circumstances:

- You face an array of annoyances over a day.
- You regularly deal with tense people.
- You face demanding time schedules.
- You work with unclear and seemingly unresolvable problems.

LTIO: Do these last statements sound like your life in your role as a CSR? What is the challenge of living in this ongoing barrage of stress?

_____

_____

_____

LEARNING POINT: You can decide to make your stress levels work for you—not against you.

Notes:

_____

_____

_____

_____

_____

_____

_____

_____

_____

ACTIVITY
84

When Do I Feel Stressed?

Everybody feels stressed under different circumstances. Some people do scary activities—such as climbing mountain peaks or jumping off them. Some people are excited about speaking in front of large audiences. Others would rather die than do that. We could go on with hundreds of such examples.

Some people can stand next to an angry customer who is yelling at them and remain cool as cucumbers. Others want to run away and never again take a job where customers feel justified to attack.

We are all different and have varied responses to events. We can all learn how to better tolerate events that cause us stress.

LTIO: In what situations do you feel stressed? Think of a mix of examples from work and your personal life.

1. _____

2. _____

3. _____

4. _____

In what situations does your stress stimulate you so your performance improves? Be as specific as you can. Use examples from your work and your personal life.

1. _____

2. _____

3. _____

LEARNING POINT: You are unique in your stress response. No one is quite like you.

Notes:

_____

_____

_____

_____

_____

_____

_____

_____

_____

_____

_____

_____

_____

85

How Does Stress Affect My Performance?

One of the biggest prices we pay for mismanaged stress is poor performance. We're sluggish, tired, unfocused, and perhaps restless, and we procrastinate about everything.

With hypostress, we have difficulty gearing ourselves up for a task. With hyperstress, it's difficult to channel our nerves. In the latter, we forget things, have difficulty concentrating, make more mistakes, and get tired. We probably don't feel good about ourselves either.

With optimum stress, we are exhilarated; we are able to process information quickly, we're efficient, and our production levels are high. We don't get exhausted from everything we do. This chart illustrates the relationship between stress and performance, where the highest level of performance operates in the middle of the curve.

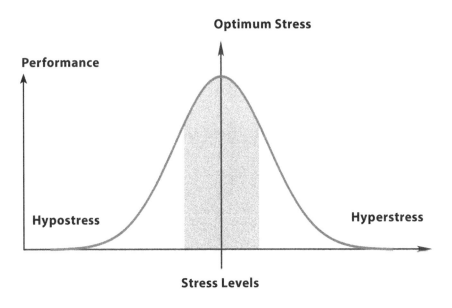

LTIO: How much stress energy do you need to take care of your customers? In comparison, what kind of events would be on the hypo- or hyperstress sides?

On the chart below, indicate what activities you perform throughout your day, both at work and in your personal life. Arrange the tasks according to the energy necessary to accomplish them.

Tasks that belong on the left-hand side require minimal effort. Tasks on the right-hand side are those that cause you to feel hyperstressed. Which tasks do you perform that are in the optimum stress portion of this chart? These tasks require effort and concentration but not excessive energy. You can do this type of task for extended periods of time. You find these tasks energizing and stimulating, but they do not overload you. Your highest level of performance operates in the middle of this curve.

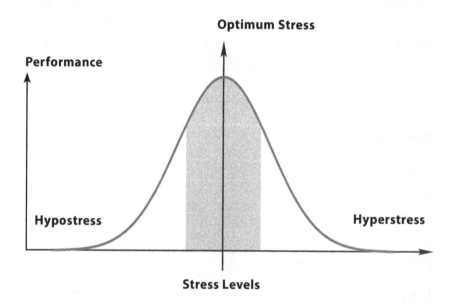

Complaint-handling tasks that leave me in the hypostress zone:

_____

_____

_____

_____

I need more stress to perform well at these tasks. One way I can do that is to set deadlines or quality standards that require me to put in more effort.

Complaint-handling tasks where I perform at an optimal level:

_____

_____

_____

_____

It would be great if I could learn to spend most of my day at work here!

Complaint-handling tasks that put me in the hyperstress zone:

_____

_____

_____

_____

I need to relax a bit to perform well at these tasks. I can do that by learning new complaint-handling techniques or taking short breaks when I become overwhelmed or stressed.

86

Stress Signals

Taking care of complaining customers is not easy. To have the energy and strength to do this, we need to take care of ourselves so we are in peak form.

What is difficult about stress is that we must have enough stimulation to make us productive but not so much pressure that it paralyzes us or takes us to the breaking point, a state called burnout. Too much stress can wreak havoc not only on our bodies but also on our relationships.

Our bodies are intelligent. They send us signals when we are getting to the burnout state. There are four types of signals:

- *Physical*—Headaches, back pain, upset stomach, diarrhea, nausea, skin rashes, elevated pulse, insomnia, unexplained acute pain, ongoing fatigue, difficulty breathing, ulcers, clenched jaw, tense muscles, sweaty palms, dark circles under the eyes, or frequent minor illnesses, such as flu or colds.
- *Mental*—Forgetfulness, inability to concentrate, mistake prone, confusion, spacing out, less rational thinking, poor judgment, decreased performance.
- *Emotional*—Mood swings, depression, apathy, unexplained sudden anger or sadness, nonspecific anxiety, panic attacks, feeling overwhelmed, nervous laughter, or verbal tics.
- *Behavioral*—Excessive use of alcohol or smoking, eating a lot or not eating, yelling, fidgeting, being easily irritated, talking too much, starting nervous habits such as nail-biting, insomnia,

avoidance behaviors, or compulsive behaviors such as shopping or cleaning.

It may seem as if these are four long lists of signals. In reality, these signals are just a few of the multiple ways humans show stress.

LTIO: Write down your own signals in the chart below. You can start with the lists above and then write any additional ones you know are your stress signals.

Type of signal	My stress signals
Physical	
Mental	
Emotional	
Behavioral	

Notes:

_____

_____

_____

_____

_____

_____

What Are My Stress Signals?

LTIO: Show your list from activity 86 to someone you know well and ask if you have any other signals you might not be aware of but that they can see. For example, your face might turn red, and you haven't noticed that. Or perhaps you bite your knuckles or fingernails when you are stressed.

Choose two examples from each type of signal that you will pay particular attention to and write the below. Perhaps you can highlight them so they will stand out on this page. Remember, these stress signals are your friends. In some way, it's your body complaining to you and giving you a gift.

Whenever you notice one of your signals, stop, and say to yourself, "Is this going to help whatever I am doing?" For example, is biting your fingernails going to help you talk with an upset complaining customer? Probably not.

Tell yourself to stop engaging in that behavior. By bringing your signals to awareness, you have a chance to stop doing them.

Notes:

Physical: _____

Mental: _____

Emotional: _____

Behavioral: _____

ACTIVITY

88

What Are My Stressors?

Stressors are the things happening around us that cause us to respond. These can be social, economic, political, family, and interpersonal. There are hundreds of events that cause us to respond. We will look at just one category of stressors: our job and career stressors. You will find on our web page a document that has a complete list of all the other hundreds of stressors: www.ciag.online/88. Use that list to identify any of your other stressors.

LTIO: Put a check beside the job and career stressors that you know affect you. Then highlight the most important ones for you.

- ☐ Communication misunderstandings
- ☐ Hostile customers
- ☐ High expectations of management
- ☐ Time wasters such as meaningless forms that must be filled out
- ☐ Lack of appreciation for your work
- ☐ Boredom
- ☐ Not enough breaks
- ☐ Low compensation
- ☐ Responsibility without control
- ☐ Incompetent coworkers
- ☐ Too many meetings
- ☐ Physical environment
- ☐ Customers who swear

- ☐ Lack of job training
- ☐ Customers waiting on hold for you
- ☐ Equipment failures
- ☐ Conflicts with coworkers
- ☐ Office politics
- ☐ Personal failures

Add any others below:

- ☐ _____
- ☐ _____
- ☐ _____
- ☐ _____
- ☐ _____
- ☐ _____
- ☐ _____
- ☐ _____

89

Burnout—Is This Me?

Since first described almost fifty years ago, *burnout* has become a widely used term. Sociologists and psychologists originally used the term to refer to those who had careers in health care, psychological counseling, or childcare.

In today's economy, burnout has been applied to essential workers. It's caused by the stress that comes from serving other people—especially under tight deadlines. It's easy to see how burnout can affect complaint handlers.

It's a syndrome that includes exhaustion, cynicism, and loss of motivation. People who are burned out feel emotionally exhausted. When that happens, they think they can no longer help others. And we all know how much emotions are intertwined with complaint handling.

There are generally three strong recognized signals of burnout. The chart below shows additional signals, but three are serious signals: (1) lack of motivation, (2) fatigue that doesn't go away, and (3) a cynical attitude about things that matter. It's easy to see how these signals will affect your performance.

It's also easy to see how burnout can become almost commonplace—especially in fields where interaction with people is intense. When this happens, CSRs readily become angry and might shout, "I'm not taking this anymore. I quit." That's not a fun place to be, and quitting was probably far from their minds when they first became a CSR.

Burnout doesn't occur after one tough day. That's just a high-stress day. You go home in the evening (or get off your computer at home), and by the next morning you are ready to go again. We've all had days like that. Burnout is caused by a number of these days, one after another, perhaps week after week, and no relief in sight.

LTIO: In the following table, put a checkmark by any of the burnout signals that apply to you.

Burnout is caused by chronic workplace stress and begins to show up in many ways. The following self-assessment will enable you to see where you are on the burnout scale.

Where do you fall on a scale from 1 to 5?

1 = "This isn't me at all."
2 = "This is me—rarely."
3 = "Occasionally I experience this factor."
4 = "A good description of me quite a bit of the time."
5 = "This pretty well describes me all the time."

Factor	1–5	Description
1. Lack of motivation		
2. Constant worries		
3. Reduced work performance		
4. Fatigue that doesn't go away		
5. Strong mood swings		
6. Can't concentrate		
7. Fighting about even small things		
8. Cynical attitude about things that matter		
9. Sleep problems		
10. Stop taking care of myself		

Interpret your score:

10–20: low stress
21–30: manageable
31–40: high stress
41–50: burnout

If you scored as having high stress, it's important to lower your stress. We will talk about some techniques to achieve that in the following pages. If your score is above forty, we suggest you contact health services in your organization.

90

Short Relaxation Techniques

Sometimes stress feels like a constant force, as if our brains have gone haywire. Stress may feel unstoppable. This type of stress is best brought under control with small, quick techniques. It's true that at times we need to take an extended period of relaxation to bring our stress under control. Other times, small breaks can work miracles; in fact, they may work better than extended meditation. The next two exercises described below are examples of short, quick techniques that can be done multiple times throughout the day.

Circuit Breakers

You can do circuit breakers throughout the day. The technique helps break the circuit of stress, and then you can move on with your day with less stress. On the following web page you will find two videos where Janelle explains what they are: www.ciag.online/90.

LTIO: After watching the two videos, what did you learn?

1. _____

2. _____

3. _____

LTIO: What circuit breakers will you use? Please choose five circuit breaker cues. Whenever you notice your cue, take in a deep breath of air and say, "I am relaxed." Then continue on with your day. You can track your use of circuit breaker cues on the chart below.

Circuit breaker cue	How is this cue working for you?
1.	
2.	
3.	
4.	
5.	

Neck Relaxation

In addition to your shoulders getting stiff, when you are seated for long periods of time, your neck is probably getting tight as well.

This exercise takes less than a minute to do, and if done whenever you notice your neck getting tight or on a regular basis a couple of times a day, you will experience much looser neck muscles. This exercise can be done while you are talking on the phone—no special equipment required.

LTIO: Count numbers with your nose. Sit in a comfortable position. Your eyes can be open or closed, depending on your activity. Some people say they get dizzy if they do this exercise with their eyes closed, so decide what's best for you.

1. Draw the numbers 1, 2, 3, 4, 5, 6, 7, 8, 9, 0 in the air with your nose.
2. Draw the numbers large and make your movements slow.
3. Don't strain. Be careful not to pull against tight muscles or to force your head too far backwards.

This activity takes about a minute to do and can be done several times a day. Most people who practice with that kind of regularity report a marked reduction in shoulder and neck tension. Some people even report a lessening or elimination of tension headaches.

This technique will work for any joint in your body. For example, some soccer players draw numbers in the air with their ankles to loosen their ankle joints. If you move slowly, you can do the same thing with your pelvis, and you'll find your lower back will loosen. Put your hands against a wall, lean with your body, and make the number movements with your hips.

Notes:

_____

_____

_____

_____

_____

_____

_____

_____

Mindfulness and the Raisin Technique

Mindfulness is one of the latest buzzwords in organizations. It has to do with being fully present and placing focused awareness on your body and surroundings while quieting down distractions that might overwhelm you. It's a proven way to achieve these six results when handling complaints.

1. *Less stress*—To decrease stress is one of the primary reasons why people practice mindfulness.
2. *Focus*—By really listening and being aware of your own emotions, you can be objective and focus on what the customer needs or wants instead of your internal dialogue.
3. *Empathy*—By paying attention to your own space, you can develop a greater understanding of what the customer needs.
4. *More creativity*—Cookie-cutter solutions can't solve all problems. Sometimes you need to look outside the box for solutions. Mindfulness increases creative capacity.
5. *Improved memory*—By being completely in the present, you can help remember more of what customers tell you.
6. *Better health*—As we have seen, less stress means that your brain and body work in a better, healthier way. Consistently practicing mindfulness over a period of time improves your brain's ability to process information, make decisions, form memories, and improve attention.

If you could improve yourself in the above six areas, wouldn't it be worth your time to spend ten minutes or so a day just sitting quietly and paying attention to your breathing and your body?

LEARNING POINT: Mindfulness isn't something magical. It's being in the here and now—a place most of us don't spend a lot of time!

We recommend trying the following raisin technique used by many mindfulness trainers.[1] It involves all the senses and will give you a good introduction to mindfulness.

LTIO: Before this exercise, wash your hands. Sit in a comfortable chair with no distractions. Put a plate with a few raisins on it next to you. If you don't like raisins, you can use any small, dried fruit or nut.

1. Put one raisin in your hand and close your eyes.
2. Feel the raisin in your hand, noticing the texture, the crevices, the size, and how it moves in your hand.
3. Put the raisin next to your ear and listen for any sounds when you squeeze it lightly. Concentrate on the raisin.
4. Put the raisin next to your nostrils. How does the raisin smell? Take a deep breath and smell the raisin again. How would you describe that smell?
5. Put the raisin in your mouth. Play with it by moving it around. See if the flavor changes as you put it in different parts of your mouth. Don't bite it; play with it until it starts falling apart. Enjoy the flavor.
6. As you swallow the raisin, imagine the journey from your mouth to your stomach. When it gets to your stomach, picture it glowing. Sense how the light makes you feel good, relaxed, and calm. Sit still for a minute or two, and then open your eyes.

How do you feel? More relaxed? If not, try it with another raisin or a nut. This time you can use the following to guide you through the exercise as you relax with your eyes closed: www.ciag.online/91.

ACTIVITY

92

The Power of Gratitude

Psychology studies tell us that showing gratitude benefits our mental health. When expressed, showing gratitude helps reduce our stress levels. It also helps in supporting solid relationships. When you say "Thank you," your body secretes endorphins that make you feel good. Even if the other person says nothing in response, you feel better by showing gratitude.

We can even be grateful when we are faced with an aggressive complainer. To help you stop your judgments that naturally arise when confronting hostility, one of the best steps to take is to distract yourself by instead focusing on the information being given to you. Consider the banana. To eat a banana, you need to take the peel off. The peel is bitter and hard to swallow. The same thing happens with complaints. We must look underneath any bitterness and examine the gift we are being given.

LTIO: What are you thankful for? Write down all the things you feel grateful for when they happen. Here are a few prompts to get you started:

I'm grateful when a customer complains, even if they are hostile, because _____

When I receive personal feedback because _____

When someone corrects me because _____

For my family and friends because _____

Showing gratitude costs nothing, and it is one of the most valuable ways to enrich the lives of yourself and others. Say your gratitude out loud so others hear it.

LTIO: Who isn't hearing from you, "I'm grateful for you being in my life?" Is there anybody you should tell how grateful you are for knowing them?

Who deserves thanks from you?	Why?	When will you tell them?

Notes:

_____

_____

_____

_____

_____

_____

_____

_____

_____

_____

ACTIVITY

93

Apps and Other Online Resources

There are many apps you can use to help reduce your stress levels. Most of these apps are free or include a free trial.

LTIO: We encourage you to try different ones until you find the one that works best for you.

- *Happify*—This brain-training app is based on research showing that activity can help you combat negativity, anxiety, and stress to foster positive traits like gratitude and empathy.
- *The Mindfulness App*—This app has five guided meditations, with options for listening to calming music or nature sounds.
- *Headspace*—This app offers a series of guided meditation sessions and mindfulness training.
- *Breathe2Relax*—This app helps you breathe better, especially focusing on diaphragmatic breathing, which can help lower stress. It also has interesting information about the effects of stress on the body.
- *My Mood Tracker*—This app helps you become more aware of what you're feeling during different events. As you track your emotions, you can manage them better.
- *Pacifica*—This app helps you through guided deep breathing and muscle relaxation exercises; it also has a mood tracker. You can record your thoughts and map out your thinking patterns.
- *GPS for the Soul*—Created by Deepak Chopra and Arianna Huffington, this app uses biofeedback to help you measure

your level of stress and monitor how you can relax by using meditation tools, calming music, and pictures.

- *Stress Doctor*—This app has a heart-rate monitor to measure the effects of calming breathing exercises in real time.
- *Pocket Yoga*—This app offers yoga poses and routines and includes many levels of difficulty.
- *Pay It Forward*—This app shows the link between generosity and reduced stress. You can program daily acts of kindness.

SELF-CHECK: Making Stress Work for Me

Why is it important for you to track your stress levels throughout the day?

1. _____

2. _____

3. _____

Which of these stress management ideas worked best for you? Are you willing to try to go back and find the ones you didn't do and try them now?

_____

_____

_____

What are your most important stress signals to track as you perform your work as a CSR?

1. _____

2. _____

3. _____

4. _____

5. _____

CHAPTER 13

Giving and Receiving
Personal Feedback

When our customers give us feedback in the form of complaints, we have a chance to learn from them. If we handle their complaint well, we also have an opportunity to strengthen our relationship with them.

Why shouldn't this apply to our personal relationships as well? If we don't speak up, our relationships may break and end. Not saying anything could be a big mistake.

94

Why Provide Feedback?

We have stated that complaints and feedback are both gifts, even though our emphasis has been on complaints. When we refer to feedback, we are telling a person that something needs to improve or change. It's not positive feedback, which we call recognition.

We consider all feedback to be positive as it can alert you to valuable information. Imagine if you never gave feedback to your children, spouse, colleagues, or employees. What would happen?

LTIO: Do you like giving feedback? Yes_____ No_____
Why?

_____

_____

_____

What bothers you the most about providing feedback?

1. _____

2. _____

3. _____

Sometimes we are not good at giving feedback. We are too aggressive, too passive, confusing, or indirect. In all these cases, feedback becomes more of a problem than a gift. The person receiving it may get angry, and then we have a self-fulfilling prophecy that feedback destroys relationships, so we stop providing feedback. But not delivering feedback also destroys relationships. What should we do? We can learn to deliver feedback in a constructive way.

LTIO: Who do you need to deliver feedback to that you haven't? Will silence fix the problem? What is the cost of not saying what you think? Let's learn how to deliver feedback constructively. In the next activity, we suggest ten ideas to deliver constructive feedback.

Notes:

_____

_____

_____

_____

_____

_____

_____

_____

_____

_____

_____

_____

_____

_____

_____

_____

_____

ACTIVITY

95

Guidelines for Providing Feedback

Simple ideas are sometimes the best to follow for helping people develop and grow. The following ideas are easy to implement and maintain respect for the person to whom you are giving feedback.

1. *Don't give feedback in front of others.*—Wait until you can schedule a time to talk with that person one on one.

2. *Ask for permission.*—People can better hear feedback if they know it is coming. Telling them prepares the brain. Don't say, "Can I give you some feedback?" This only creates stress. Instead say, "Hey, can we talk about what happened at my party?" Then wait for the yes or the approval of the other person. Don't just drop the feedback on top of them. If the person says this is not a good time, don't take it as a rejection. It's good to know the feedback probably will not be taken well at that moment. Ask, "When would be a good time for us to talk?"

3. *Check your mindset and emotions.*—Make sure you have the right mindset and emotions when providing feedback. If you are angry, even if you planned every word, your comments probably would sound aggressive. Reduce your stress. Use a stress ball, listen to music, or anything that can calm you down. Your mindset should be "How can I help this person change so I can create a better relationship with them?" or "How can I add value with my feedback?" and not "How can I make them feel bad?"

4. *Ask questions.*—Once you have their agreement to talk, then ask questions. Many times, we just go directly to what we want to get off our chest instead of asking the other person *first* what they

feel or think. Maybe that person will tell you exactly what was on your mind. For example, instead of saying, "I think it was rude of you to interrupt in front of my guests. It made me feel put down," ask, "How do you think the party went?" or "How did you like the way the conversation went? What about your behavior? I honestly thought you interrupted me quite a bit. How did you feel? How do you think others felt?"

5. *Speak in your own voice.*—Do not say, "Somebody asked me about how I could stand all the interrupting you did." When you start this way, what do you think happens next? Immediately, you lose focus to discuss what you want to say. The person you are providing feedback will ask, "Who told you?"

   The situation grows only more dire if your information is not accurate. They will say, "Who is spreading all this gossip?" If you are not sure about what happened, it's better to ask questions. Hopefully the person will acknowledge what occurred.

6. *Do not use the "sandwich" technique.*—This old technique says you must start your feedback with something positive. Then sandwich in the negative things you have to say, and finally close with a positive statement. This advice isn't good because most everyone knows the sandwich technique. Once the person you are providing feedback to hears a positive statement, they start waiting for the negative, which is the whole point of the feedback. Instead, praise someone when you need to, deliver the feedback constructively when you have to, but don't mix the two. Finishing with a positive comment after the negative is useless as it takes power away from what you just said and what the person needs to work on.

7. *Ask about the impact of their behavior on you or others.*—Once the person has recognized what they did, it's important they understand why you want them to change their behavior. A good way to do that is to ask about the impact of their behavior: for example, "What do you think was the impact on me when you

interrupted me at my dinner gathering?" This helps them grow as they realize the effect of their behaviors not just on you but others as well.

8. *Ask leading questions.*—If the person doesn't see the effect of their behavior, ask leading questions, such as "Can you see why I get annoyed when you interrupt me in front of others?"

9. *End with "What's next."*—Ask questions such as "What can I count on from you?" or "I don't want to have this situation happen again. What can we both do to make sure it doesn't? Our friendship is too important to me to go through this again."

10. *Review and reinforce.*—When you meet again, ask, "How are we doing? Are you okay with how we're communicating now?"

LTIO: With these ten ideas, you're ready to deliver constructive feedback, so let's practice!

Write the names of four people you will deliver feedback to, the topic, by when, and what happened.

Person you will give feedback to	Topic of feedback	When?	Results?

Be Specific When Giving Feedback

When delivering feedback, let the person know what your feedback conversation will be about. Help them be prepared to learn from your feedback and not be stressed.

If someone asks you, "Can I give you some feedback?" or they say directly, "I have a concern," make sure to ask specifically what it's about. In this way, you can be prepared to accept the feedback as a gift and not as a stressor.

LTIO: Read the examples below and indicate what might be said in each case so the person receiving the feedback is best prepared to hear and grow from what you want to say.

Example 1—A coworker sitting close by you noisily chews her gum. It drives you crazy. You can't concentrate, and you think it's not professional to be chewing gum while taking calls from customers. You would like to suggest she change this habit. How do you tell her you'd like to talk with her about "something" so she'll be open-minded when you talk?

_____

_____

_____

Example 2—You are on a committee of CSRs looking into how your company can learn about recurring problems. You have been charged with leading the group, but another member of your committee is bossy and acting as if they are in charge. You want to let this person know the impact this is having on you and the committee. How will you let this person know specifically what you will be discussing so they will be open-minded when you talk with them?

_____

_____

_____

Notes:

_____

_____

_____

_____

_____

_____

_____

_____

_____

_____

_____

_____

ACTIVITY

97

Taking in Personal Feedback

When someone gives you feedback, use the Gift Formula. There are additional ideas that will help you feel more comfortable when receiving personal feedback.

LTIO: Put a check in the box next to each suggestion that you are likely to try.

- ☐ *Reschedule*—Set another time if you are upset or not ready to receive feedback. You can always say, "Your feedback is very important to me, and I want to be 100 percent focused. Unfortunately, I have to run to another meeting right now. Can we meet later today?"
- ☐ *Actively listen*—Listen with all your senses and focus. It's a good idea to take notes and ask questions to clarify. Get as much out of this feedback, and it will become an even better gift.
- ☐ *Don't interrupt*—Sometimes interrupting is a way to deal with your emotions. Remember, there are two ways to interrupt: verbally and nonverbally. Nonverbally, you can make faces, let yourself get distracted, or sigh. If you need to say something, wait, be patient, breathe, and focus on what the person is saying.
- ☐ *Don't get defensive or attack*—Don't say, "Well, you do it too!" These comments don't help and will only lead to an argument and probably not getting feedback in the future. It might sometimes be difficult, but look for the pearl in the oyster.

- [ ] *Talk about next steps*—Tell the person giving you feedback how you will improve and do things differently next time. Make a commitment to follow up on it.
- [ ] *Use the Gift Formula*—We've already said this, but it doesn't hurt to repeat this suggestion. Be grateful for the feedback, and tell the person why you are grateful.

Notes:

_____

_____

_____

_____

_____

_____

_____

_____

_____

_____

_____

_____

_____

_____

_____

_____

How to Get More Personal Feedback

Some people seem to get a lot of feedback and grow from it. Other people have a reputation that you better not say anything critical, or you'll pay a price. How do you get more feedback? What do these people do? Here are four ideas.

1. *Seek out feedback*—Don't wait to receive feedback. A good way to let others know you want feedback that will help you improve is to ask for it. You'll also be more prepared to receive feedback if you ask for it.
2. *Ask for help if you need it*—If you need help, it's a good idea to go to specific people and ask for feedback. They'll appreciate being involved in your improvement.
3. *Develop a reputation*—Become known as someone who wants feedback. Let that be your brand.
4. *Do it*—Be accountable and do what you promised to do once you receive feedback. No excuses. People will tell you more if they see you are using what they say.

LTIO: Ask for feedback from three people you know who will give it to you directly and honestly. Choose a topic about which you would like this feedback. Write down who you are going to ask, by when, and state what happened.

Whom you will ask for feedback	When	Results
1.		
2.		
3.		

Notes:

_____

_____

_____

_____

_____

_____

_____

_____

_____

_____

_____

_____

_____

_____

_____

ACTIVITY

99

Setting Limits to Feedback

You don't have to accept whatever feedback is given to you. It's important to know your limits and then communicate them. Setting limits lets your family, friends, coworkers, and even bosses know your feedback limits.

Setting limits has to do with knowing the limits of your emotional space. When your space has been violated, you probably know that. If you aren't clear with your boundaries, there's a good chance your space will be violated again.

LTIO: Here are two examples, one at work and one in your personal life. There are no right or wrong answers; it's a question of what is acceptable to you. If someone speaks to you privately, that may be okay; the same feedback blurted out in front of a group may be unacceptable. Remember your space limits may shift depending on the circumstances. For each of the situations below, indicate what your limits are.

1. *At work*—English is not your native language, and you have a slight accent. None of your callers have any difficulty understanding you—just the person sitting next to you, who can hear your calls. Once again, this person is criticizing your accent. What can you say to stop them from repeatedly bringing this up?

_____

_____

_____

2. *In your personal life*—You are not skinny nor overweight. A good friend who is ultrathin keeps telling you that you would be more successful if you lost fifteen pounds. You feel comfortable with your weight and have no interest in going on a diet. How do you communicate that you don't want to discuss the topic again?

_____

_____

_____

Remember, feedback is good—even if it still hurts to hear someone else's feedback. However, sometimes the sting is too painful. But it still helps to use the Gift Formula.

Notes:

_____

_____

_____

_____

_____

_____

_____

_____

_____

_____

_____

100

The Gift Formula Works for Personal Feedback

You probably know the three-step Gift Formula by heart at this point. You can get even more practice using it by going through it when someone gives you feedback. Let's review it by changing it to be appropriate when you are receiving personal feedback.

1. Respond by building rapport.
   a. Whenever anyone gives you feedback, first say, "Thank you."
   b. Briefly state why you are glad to receive the feedback: "Thanks for telling me about that," "Thanks for pointing that out. I didn't know that irritated you," or "Thanks. I've been trying to stop doing that for some time, so thanks for speaking up."
   c. If the feedback is about something you did that hurt someone or created problems at work, apologize. All you have to say is two simple words: "I'm sorry." If the feedback is about something major, then add more words: "I'm sorry, there's no excuse for that. Please forgive me."
   d. Tell them what you are going to do.

In many instances, with personal feedback, those first three steps are all that is required. But, if more is needed, then:

2. Recover by fixing your behavior.
   a. Ask for more information about what you can do. Sometimes this is difficult when we are talking about personal feedback. You may hear all sorts of things that are difficult to hear.
   b. Make any changes you need to do as quickly as you can.
   c. Follow up. At some point, you should check back with the person who gave you the feedback and ask if they have seen any improvements. Also ask if there is anything else you need to work on.

3. Make it right so it doesn't happen again.
   a. Be accountable.
   b. Make sure your behavior changes become habitual.

Notes:

_____

_____

_____

_____

_____

_____

_____

_____

_____

_____

_____

_____

_____

ACTIVITY

101

Test Your Knowledge of the Gift Formula

We have made a special video for you in which we give feedback to each other and then ask you to criticize how we used the Gift Formula. You now have a level of expertise that you can demonstrate in your critique. Then we each use the Gift Formula and show an improved version of our responses. Point out the differences between the two videos.

LTIO: Watch the four videos at www.ciag.online/101 and answer the questions below.

Video 1: Did Victoria apply the Gift Formula when she received feedback from Janelle? Yes ___ No ___ Mostly ___ What could she have done better?

_____

_____

_____

Video 2: How did Victoria improve at using the Gift Formula in Video 2?

_____

_____

_____

Video 3: Did Janelle apply the Gift Formula when she received feedback from Victoria? Yes ___ No ___ Mostly ___ Which steps did she use? What could she have done better?

_____

_____

_____

Video 4: How did Janelle improve at using the Gift Formula in video 4?

_____

_____

_____

If you can see what both Janelle and Victoria did in videos 1 and 3 that could have been done better, and you can see the improvements in videos 2 and 4, then you learned a lot about the Gift Formula. Congratulations for completing 101 activities.

Notes:

_____

_____

_____

_____

_____

_____

_____

_____

SELF-CHECK: Giving and Receiving Personal Feedback

Why do you suppose feedback is so difficult to receive? What can you personally do to focus on the gifts you receive?

_____

_____

_____

Why is feedback so difficult to give in a way that the other person can learn and grow and your relationship can get stronger? What can you personally do to get better at giving feedback?

_____

_____

_____

What kind of a world do you think this would be if we all learned how to better take in feedback and give helpful feedback, and do it in such a way that people see the gift that is being given to them? Draw a picture!

Next Steps

Wow! You did it. You've gone through this workbook. Congratulate yourself! We congratulate you! We know it isn't easy to conduct your daily work obligations and cover a topic as large as complaint handling. As you have no doubt discovered, the matter of complaint handling is a gigantic subject. It touches and is touched by many related business topics.

You can't do everything. The critical question right now is, What are your next steps? Below you'll find some ideas you can easily follow.

- *Follow a rough pathway*—If you read this book while using a highlighter, you can probably see a rough pathway of ideas that will continue to reinforce the A Complaint Is a Gift mindset. That pathway would include repeating the concepts and techniques that you will follow until they become second nature to you.
- *Appreciate the value of the CIAG mindset*—You have no doubt figured out that your mindset affects you, your customers, and your colleagues. Every time you practice the techniques and ideas you intend to make part of your complaint-handling process, you will also be reinforcing the A Complaint Is a Gift mindset. And that's a decisive step, no matter how you do it.

- *Consider your role in your organization*—Part of your next steps will depend on your role in your organization. We are mostly writing these next steps for individual CSRs. As a CSR, you are probably more interested in focusing on how to deal with complaining customers. Managers will want to encourage their CSRs to practice the best complaint-handling techniques in this workbook. Leaders of organizations should look to create a service recovery map. We encourage managers and leaders to acquire *A Complaint Is a Gift*, third edition. It covers some of the same topics in greater depth and introduces relevant ideas to your leadership positions.
- *Keep practicing the Gift Formula*—A careful reading of chapter four will teach you about the Gift Formula, and its practice will anchor the concept of the *A Complaint Is a Gift* book and this workbook. It's a central focus of this book. Once you have developed a habit of always thanking others for their feedback, you've got the basics.
- *Review your progress on this complete CIAG topic*—Return to the workbook from time to time (perhaps once a month) and glance at the answers that you shared here. It's easy to forget that complaints are gifts after dealing with a string of difficult customers.
- *Complete the activities in the chapter on difficult customers*—Most CSRs have some customers who are challenging. Some CSRs have a lot. But everybody will face challenging feedback and complaints at one time or another. It's good to be prepared.
- *Be ready to be empathetic*—It's challenging to turn empathy on or off like a switch. Be ready to develop your empathy so it's constantly there. Learn to recognize the six basic emotional displays we all make on our faces—everywhere worldwide.
- *Keep practicing your questioning and listening skills*—This will help you in all parts of your life. They work particularly well in the field of complaint handling.

- *Continue studying body language*—There is so much going on when someone complains, whether in our personal or business lives. Learn how to read the subtle language that the truth of our bodies communicate.
- *Choose powerful phrases and make them your friends*—We provided you with pages of powerful phrases. No doubt there are several that are not part of your everyday lexicon. Start using them. Once you find yourself saying them without thinking, add a couple more. They are powerful!
- *Take care of yourself*—Customer service is not easy work. It takes energy, and without a strong body to move through your day, you run the risk of burning out. Nobody wins when that happens. But it's not necessary to become overstressed. It's a decision you make to take care of yourself. We wish that for you.
- *Pay attention to giving and receiving personal feedback*—Feedback helps us grow, just as complaints help businesses improve. Most of the ideas from this workbook are as relevant to our business life as our personal life. Start saying "Thank you" to everyone who offers you feedback. You'll be amazed how it reduces people's fights with each other.

Complaints involve emotional intelligence that must be applied to each unique transaction with another person. With a well-established mindset about complaints, you can appreciate how the complex nature of complaint handling requires a broad understanding of emotions. It is lifelong learning because psychologists continue to reveal a deeper knowledge of human interactions. This continuous learning is part of your individual next steps in the world of complaint handling.

Notes

Chapter 4

1. Astrid Pocklington, "Customer Complaints: Are They a Curse or a Blessing?" *Forbes*, September 3, 2020, https://www.forbes.com/sites /forbescommunicationscouncil/2020/09/03/customer-complaints-are -they-a-curse-or-a-blessing/?sh=7348363d6ea3.

2. Mary Jo Bitner, Bernard H. Booms, and Mary Stanfield Tetreault, "The Service Encounter: Diagnosing Favorable and Unfavorable Incidents," *Journal of Marketing* 54, no. 1 (January 1990): 71–84.

Chapter 5

1. Dialog Direct and Customer Care Measurement and Consulting, *The Customer Rage Study: An Independent Study of Customer Complaint-Handling Experiences* (Highland Park, MI: Dialog Direct, 2016), 14.

2. Carol Hymowitz, "Everyone Likes to Laud Serving the Customer; Doing It Is the Problem," *Wall Street Journal*, February 27, 2006, https://www.wsj.com/articles/SB114099856509483777.

3. Peter C. Hill, Julie Juola Exline, and Adam B. Cohen, "The Social Psychology of Justice and Forgiveness in Civil and Organizational Settings," in *Handbook of Forgiveness*, ed. Everett L. Worthington Jr. (New York: Taylor and Francis, 2005), 477–490.

4. Norma Gutierrez, as quoted in Charlotte Klopp and John Sterlicchi, "Customer Satisfaction Just Catching On in Europe, *Marketing News* 24, no. 11 (May 28, 1990): 5.

5. Roland Zahn et al., "The Neural Basis of Human Social Values: Evidence from Functional MRI," *Cerebral Cortex* 19, no. 2 (February 2009): 276–283, https://www.ncbi.nlm.nih.gov/pmc/articles/PMC2733324/.

Chapter 6

1. Carl Rogers, "Empathic: An Unappreciated Way of Being," *Counseling Psychologist* 5, no. 2 (June 1975): 2–10.

2. "Smiles from 300 Feet Away," Blue Wave Orthodontics, September 30, 2014, https://bluewaveortho.com/Blog/smiles-from-300-feet-away/; and Maria Guarnea et al., "Facial Expressions and Ability to Recognize Emotions from Eyes or Mouth in Children," *European Journal of Psychology* 11, no. 2 (May 2015): 183–196.

3. Paul Ekman, E. Richard Sorenson, and Wallace V. Friesen, "Pan-cultural Elements in the Facial Displays of Emotion," *Science* (April 4, 1969): 86–88. Also see Paul Ekman, "Universal Emotions," Paul Ekman Group, https://www.paulekman.com/universal-emotions/.

Chapter 8

1. "3 Levels of Listening, When to Think, When to Focus, When to Step Back," The People Piece, n.d., https://www.peoplepiece.com/our-insights /levels-of-listening.

2. Jeffrey R. Young, "A Popular Study Found That Taking Notes by Hand Is Better Than by Laptop. But Is It?" *EdSurge Podcast*, April 27, 2021, https:// www.edsurge.com/news/2021-04-27-a-popular-study-found-that -taking-notes-by-hand-is-better-than-by-laptop-but-is-it.

Chapter 11

1. See "Free Resources," Crisis and Trauma Resource Institute, https://ca.ctrinstitute.com/resources/.

Chapter 12

1. See Christine Webb, "How a Raisin Can Help You with Mindfulness," *Netdoctor*, September 30, 2016, https://www.netdoctor.co.uk/healthy-living /wellbeing/news/a27040/easy-raisin-mindfulness-exercise/.

How Trainers Can Use
This Workbook

If you are a trainer, coach, or facilitator, either external or in-company, this workbook is a great resource for you to deliver as a companion to the A Complaint Is a Gift workshop. This program has been tested with major companies over the last three decades, proving its viability.

You can use this workbook in the order presented here to support a complete complaint-handling workshop, covering the different aspects of complaint handling. You can also move the chapter contents around or skip as needed to tailor it for different audiences. You can see that the content of this workbook has a broad range, and some of the topics may already have been built into other presentations you offer.

If you would like to use our prepared PowerPoint slides, plus the trainer manual and the step-by-step guide to facilitate the exercises, please go to www.ciag.online/ttt.

You can also get certified as a CIAG facilitator by Janelle Barlow. You will find information about that on the web page as well. Victoria Holtz will offer a similar certification TTT program for Spanish speakers.

The benefits of the A Complaint Is a Gift Train the Trainer program include

- Bringing a tailored, cost-effective, follow-up solution to your company's in-depth needs for complaint handling
- Having an in-house trainer facilitator, which makes it easier to adapt the cases to examples from your own company
- Allowing trainers, facilitators, and coaches to grow and be recognized for their proven skills by taking advantage of the certification program
- Providing flexibility to choose from thirteen modules that fit your organizational needs
- Multiplying your expertise as everyone involved with complaint handling learns by attending in-company or department-wide programs
- Spreading the A Complaint Is a Gift mindset across your organization, which will help the results achieved become sustainable
- Adapting the program to hourlong sessions or full-day workshops will provide maximum flexibility
- Tapping into the lucrative market for external trainers, facilitators, or coaches
- Taking advantage of the workbook, the step-by-step guide, and the online TTT, and also accessing the bonus of monthly live sessions with us so your questions can be answered with virtual, real support

We welcome you! We know you will have a great experience as you become involved with the CIAG Train the Trainers program. Please send questions to janelle@JanelleBarlow.com or Victoria@moveminds.com.

About the Authors

Janelle Barlow, PhD, has long given up the notion that complaints will disappear as soon as companies learn to produce perfect products and services. That's not going to happen! She has come to believe that complaints will never go away; instead, they can keep customers close to you.

She has decades of experience as a global speaker, virtual presenter, and author. Her main speaking and consulting goal is to engage people to see how complaints are gifts and, with the right mindset, do not have to be overwhelming for those who listen to customer dissatisfaction.

The A Complaint Is a Gift mindset has been adopted by dozens of corporations and associations in seventy-three countries (see acomplaintisagift.com/Janelle). Many of them use her service recovery map while working to make their organizations complaint friendly.

She loves writing and designing innovative curriculum projects, and she has authored several books, including *Branded Customer Service, Emotional Value, Smart Videoconferencing*, and *A Complaint Is a Gift*, all published by Berrett-Koehler. She also wrote *The Stress Manager*, edited the book *Shift*, and created the online learning experience *Creativity: Unbind Your Mind*, with the European-based company Uninet AS.

She can be reached at Janelle@JanelleBarlow.com.

Victoria Holtz, PhD, has delivered keynotes in forty-four countries across five continents. For more than twenty-seven years, she has worked with dozens of Fortune 500 companies, including Microsoft, Nestle, Uber, Pfizer, VW, KPMG, American Express, Henkel, Cisco, Siemens, AAA, and AIG, to achieve an agile mindset culture and improve return on investment and return on people and get sustainable results.

Victoria has seen firsthand how the CIAG workshops help companies excel in the complex task of having everyone aligned and ready to make customers, suppliers, and coworkers feel that their complaints really are gifts and then use these gifts to co-create solutions so there is learning throughout the organization.

She is CEO for Moveminds Latin America, managing teams in Mexico, Colombia, Peru, Argentina, and Brazil. She was elected as a Femmes Leaders Mondiales (Women World Leaders) member, looking for more diversity and equality in the workplace, and was named Latam Head for the Global Future of Work Foundation.

She is a business transformation expert in the TV Azteca Internacional program, TransformARTE. She has also been a guest on several television programs on Discovery Health Channel, Bloomberg, Canal Once, Telemundo, Televisa, and Univision.

You can find more information about her at ciag.online.com /Victoria.

Also by Janelle Barlow

A Complaint Is a Gift

How to Learn from Critical Feedback and Recover Customer Loyalty, 3rd Edition

The bestselling *A Complaint Is a Gift* introduced the revolutionary notion that customer complaints are not annoyances but valuable feedback. They help organizations improve products and service style, focus marketing, and strengthen customer loyalty. This new edition condenses the tried-and-true eight-step Gift Formula into three tighter, more efficient steps. Based on her work with clients, Janelle Barlow has updated the industry-specific complaint examples and added new concepts, such as enabling employees to handle complaints with emotional resilience to better deal with increasingly difficult customers in the wake of the pandemic.

Paperback 978-1-5230-0293-1
PDF ebook 978-1-5230-0294-8
ePub ebook 978-1-5230-0295-5
Digital audiobook 978-1-5230-0296-2

BK Berrett–Koehler Publishers, Inc.
www.bkconnection.com

800.929.2929

Dear reader,

Thank you for picking up this book and welcome to the worldwide BK community! You're joining a special group of people who have come together to create positive change in their lives, organizations, and communities.

What's BK all about?

Our mission is to connect people and ideas to create a world that works for all.

Why? Our communities, organizations, and lives get bogged down by old paradigms of self-interest, exclusion, hierarchy, and privilege. But we believe that can change. That's why we seek the leading experts on these challenges—and share their actionable ideas with you.

A welcome gift

To help you get started, we'd like to offer you a **free copy** of one of our bestselling ebooks:

www.bkconnection.com/welcome

When you claim your **free ebook**, you'll also be subscribed to our blog.

Our freshest insights

Access the best new tools and ideas for leaders at all levels on our blog at ideas.bkconnection.com.

Sincerely,

Your friends at Berrett-Koehler